TATTERED EDGES

TATTERED EDGES

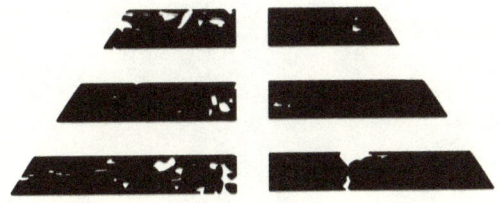

By: Marco Santucci

CITI OF
BOOKS

CITIOFBOOKS, INC.
3736 Eubank NE Suite A1
Albuquerque, NM 87111-3579
www.citiofbooks.com

Hotline: 1 (877) 389-2759
Fax: 1 (505) 930-7244

Ordering Information:
Quantity sales. Special discounts are available on quantity purchases by corporations, associations, and others. For details, contact the publisher at the address above.

Printed in the United States of America.

ISBN-13:	Softcover	978-1-959682-04-2
	eBook	978-1-959682-05-9

Library of Congress Control Number: 2022919241

For Pam,

Who was there for me, supporting and loving me unconditionally, despite the losses she suffered because of what I am and whom I've become. Thank you for traveling with me down this winding road that I've walked, which has been far more pleasant with you by my side.

— Marco

TABLE CONTENTS

INTRODUCTION

*T*here are many things in life that we fail to understand until long after we begin to ponder them. Most of these things we experience at the appropriate time in life starting with our first breath upon exiting the birth canal, with a blast of icy air engulfing our tiny bodies.

The sheer thought of relying on another person to keep us alive and kicking for the first several years of our lives is a frightening thought, especially learning that when someone, such as myself, was a baby back when car seats themselves were in their own infancy. It does make you wonder a bit about which of us are meant to be here, for how much time, and why. Everyone wants to have a purpose in life. We spend most of our life wondering just what that purpose is. Do we not? We are completely controlled by our parents in the beginning. Their core values are what will mold our life into ways we may or may not agree with as time goes on. I had great respect for my parents, something that kids these days lack greatly for the most part. There are so few now that seem to hold that kind of attitude towards not only parents, but life itself.

I was adopted as an infant in 1965 by Carmen and Dorothy Santucci. I was the second child to be adopted by them; an older brother Nick, had been two and a half years before me. My mother was unable to conceive for eleven years prior to their first adoption.

Though lo and behold, two and a half years after they adopted me, came their only natural child: my younger brother, Michael.

My father was a successful businessman as a gas station owner called Santucci's Shell, as in Shell Oil Co. Back then, they pumped the gas for you, washed your windows and serviced your car. My Grandfather, Carlo, had a music store in town, and yes, it was actually named *Santucci for Music*. He too was a very successful businessman. Born in Italy, he was the only child to survive out of five, and with polio to boot. His parents made the trek with him as a toddler to the United States, ending up in the small town of Ottawa, Illinois, in the very beginning of the 1900's. He would end up teaching himself to play the piano, violin, and the accordion.

I remember every year on Christmas day as far back as me being five years old, an envelope went to each of the grandkids from "Nono", which is Italian for Grandpa. Each envelope contained a crisp fifty-dollar bill. Every time I saw one of those it was all the money in the world as far as I was concerned, and went straight into the bank. My mother was very good about saving. I sure wish I could have followed that trend. Growing up in a small mid western town was a pretty good thing back then, and with the last name Santucci, in that town carried a lot of weight.

My mother once asked me if I remembered asking her if she would hire a detective to find my birth mother. I was nine, and I do remember that. I was six when she revealed to me that I was adopted and what that meant. She gave me a book, I no longer have, that was all about being adopted and how we are chosen. The book was written and illustrated by a friend of hers. As I became older, she told me my birth mother did love me but was not able to keep me. Almost thirty years later I would hear the truth right from my birth mother's own mouth.

As much as society is changing, some of it still remains the same; for example, the line between boys and girls. A child is born; upon quick visual inspection the child is male or female, hopefully with ten fingers and ten toes. Who would have thought there could ever be any kind of variance in something so simple? One would think that it is like comparing black and white: opposites. Now, after many years of research and many, many stories from people around the globe it has been determined that, whether society likes it or not, there is a spectrum of gender expression. I am not referring to sexual orientation at all; that is a completely different subject. This was something I had to learn myself as time went by, since I too, like most people, are taught what we are supposed to be and how one is expected to act as they go along their path in life. Before I continue, I want to say to those of you who really know me, thank you for standing by me. And to those of you, who thought you knew me, remember you never know who or what is standing right beside you.

ONE

*F*or some reason I can't seem to shake off the first and only time I recall my mom changing my little brother's diaper. I couldn't have been even five yet but it is still ingrained within my memory forever. This is not an age where we even think there are differences between anyone beyond their face. We don't think about body parts when we are so young. Why would we? We eat, sleep, pee, and poop. With my little brother lying on the foot of the bed, me at my mother's side, she began to remove his diaper. Not only did he have something I did not, but it did tricks too. It moved in an upward direction for some reason all on its own. I was perplexed to say the least. With my mother's back to him while she grabbed a fresh diaper and I imagine, wipes and powder, I decided to give it a tap to see what would happen. Every time I did, it went back to the standing position. She had then turned back and saw what I was doing and told me to stop naturally; at least she didn't overreact as one might expect.

A few years later I had witnessed my older brother going pee in our downstairs bathroom, which was the size of a large broom closet. It is where we spent most of our time if we were not outside since we had a playroom, with built-in shelves on one side and metal ones on the another which held all our toys, and later books and board games. Again, I was perplexed since he was standing to go pee. This was something I needed to try to do, because in my mind there was not really any difference between the two of us other than at the time, he was taller. After he had finished, I went in and shut the pinewood door.

The same door some years later, I would break into trying to get at him to punch him really hard. I stood at the toilet bowl looking down into it. I pulled my pants down and started to let my body do its thing. As pee began to stream down my legs, I stopped myself and moved in closer now straddling the bowl pushing harder now seemed to help the stream flow straight. This is the only memory I hold of such an incident so I will assume it didn't prove to go well enough to continue such a practice.

My mother was a meticulous woman in many respects. She kept our home spotless and her children as well. She would dress us to the T when going anywhere in public, especially on holidays. When you're a little kid what choice do you have, and you don't realize the time may come when such clothes will seem very absurd. My older brother was a cub scout. I wanted to be a cub scout too. I thought the uniform shirt was very cool with all its patches of achievements my mother had hand sewn on ever so perfectly. I would go into his side of the closet since he shared a room with my little brother, and put on that shirt and would admire myself in the mirror. I thought it looked mighty fine on me at the age of nine. I was not to ever become a cub scout. No, I was what they called a Bluebird. How stupid of a name and not very cool sounding like "cub scout". The only reason I agreed to it was so I could accumulate the achievement beads that would be sewn on to the dumb looking felt vest I had. The whole back of my vest had beads from sport activities, with no one else achieving the same level as me. This is too easy I thought. I went to a St. Columba Catholic school until the fifth grade, that's where I got involved with Bluebirds.

I thank God that my older brother got into trouble while he was in the eighth grade for taking a sharpie and marking up all the walls in a continues line, going three flights of stairs to the top of the old building. My mom told me she was transferring me to a public school for sixth grade since she felt incredible shame from my brother Nick's antics.

Why would he do such a thing? Who knows, he was a pretty strange kid. He was always small for his age, and never had many friends. What he was good at was taking things apart, and reassembling them from a very early age. He spent hours at the workbench in the basement building things with his erector set, and showing me just how incredibly cool mercury was to play with. He had chemistry sets back then; but I'm not sure if that would have been an included element in one of his kits. God knows where he would have gotten it. We never did get along, I always thought he was a bit creepy, then he proved it to me. One night downstairs while we were watching TV, he was on the couch and I was sitting in the chair to the right of him. He only wore his underwear in the summer; so, he gets my attention and flashes his dick at me hoping I would respond to his liking. What a freak; I immediately got up and went upstairs. The second time he tried that shit he came into my room and tried getting into bed with me. I started yelling, so naturally our mom came running in. He said he just wanted "Boots" my cat. I never told my mom about either incident.

By the time we were both in high school he had been running with the wrong crowd, getting high on at least marijuana, and possibly other street drugs. Nick liked to hang out at the Pool Hall. That was one of the places drug deals went down. One night Nick's connection called our house; I answered the phone and he said, "I'm going to kill your brother". "Go ahead" I responded. I know it is sad, but I really didn't care.

Naturally attending a Catholic school, at least back then, also meant going to church on a weekly basis. St. Columba's church steeple stretched beyond the eye's view from inside. I recall as I relive the memory of sitting in one of the pews that it must have been at least 100 feet to the peak. Hanging from what seemed like a mile high ceiling, were several blood-red elongated glass lanterns, like fixtures. They looked like encased candle holders and were attached to very long gold chains. I would stare at them every time I was there, engrossed in the flickering flames dancing inside. Enormous stained-glass images of the stations of the cross lined both sides of the church as most any other Catholic place of worship. I never questioned anything back then; did as I was told at home and in the church. Kneel, sit, stand, and tolerate the organ music that was dreadfully dull.

Leaving St Columba School also meant leaving that particular church. My mother was just too embarrassed by Nick's behavior, so attending a different church was in order. That was going to be St. Mary's in Naplate where my dad's gas station was located.

Naplate is considered a village to this day with its own population of no more than 400, and also where my grandfather had once been the mayor. It shares the same zip code as Ottawa, so go figure on it being separate.

1980, the year I turned fifteen was when I began to question things about the church, and religion in general. One of the days my mom and I were going to confession, I simply asked her "Why do I have to confess my sins to a man?" "He intercedes for you" she replied. I told her, "That makes no sense mom, we are supposed to have a direct line to God, and no intercession should be needed." She didn't care for my comment, and she really didn't like my thought process, so now the breakdown had begun.

One of the best things in my life was my mini bike. I had it since I was nine, and soon I would be too big for it. It was a 1969 Honda z50. They were the best things ever back then. Mine had a silver and maroon two-tone gas tank, chrome exhaust pipes and chrome folding handlebars, the light kit was removed, though I don't know why. A huge collector's item now; I must get my hands on another one, one of these days. My mother hated the fact that I rode a dirt bike; she blamed my dad that this was the reason I was the way I was for God's sake. Never mind the fact I was a good rider. My dad bought me a 1974 Honda XL 75 next and that lasted until I rode the front shocks right off of it. He bought it from Tommy Small's grandfather. His grandsons lived with him; I didn't understand that at the time. Tommy had my dream bike: a 1976 Yamaha 80, with its yellow gas tank and black trim. My heart would skip a beat when I saw it. He lived in the next subdivision where properties merged into an area that new homes were being built at the time. There was still a lot of open space in which to ride a dirt bike, and that is where Tommy rode his. I would go out there to watch since our bikes were kept at the gas station, we had to wait for the weekends to ride.

There were only a few families who moved into the new homes then, as there were a handful built at the time. One day this older kid named Jay started talking to me about dirt bikes. We walked along for a while, and then he said he had something to show me in his house. I followed him in and up the tan colored pile carpeted stairs of the two-story house. Being only twelve at the time, I wasn't thinking there might possibly be a problem with following a sixteen-year-old boy to his bedroom. Once we reached the top of the stairs, we turned left and into his room. He began babbling about a few trophies on his chest of drawers. When I turned all the way around to look at them, he came behind me and forced me to the floor. Somehow, he managed to undo my overalls and pull them and my underwear all the way down to my ankles. As I tried to fight him off, he held me down with one hand, and with the other, he unbuttoned and pulled his pants down enough to expose his massive erection. He tried with incredible force to thrust it into me.

Whether it was my overwhelming will to flee, or my guardian angel pulling me up and out of that room; I was down the stairs and out the door in seconds. I rode my bike all the way home and never said a word to anyone about it ever. When I got home, I jumped in the shower to try to scrub myself clean; I felt so defiled. All I knew at that moment was that no man would ever control me.

The summer before entering the seventh grade I got a call from Laurie Hicks; she was one of the friends I made earlier that year. We had become fast friends in the sixth grade, both being what one would call a tomboy. Not only that, we both were athletic and everyone knew it. When the Team Captains were selecting team members, Laurie and I were always the first picked. Need I say more? This was where I learned of the game we called bombardment, aka, dodgeball. I loved this game since there wasn't a ball I couldn't catch. This would carry over into junior high when our P.E. teacher, Ms. Smith, would have to blow her whistle halfway through the game and say, "Santucci, go to the other side of the court!", since I would wipe over half of them out so quickly, by catching everything thrown anywhere within five or so feet of my body. She felt it was unfair, so I needed to now become a traitor to my original team.

Laurie had called to see if I might ask my dad if he would sponsor a softball team through his business. First of all, attending a Catholic school in the 1970's offered zero sports opportunities for a girl; unless you consider cheerleading a sport. All they had was a boy's basketball team. Without hesitation, as soon as I hung up the phone receiver, I picked it up again from where it hung on the wall and called my dad to ask him if he would do this for me; not really knowing what all this entailed. As I listened intently to the phone ring, and ring, finally on the third ring I heard, "Santicci Shell, Carmen speaking". "Hi dad, would you sponsor a summer softball team for me and some other kids?", I said excitedly. His response was, "Sure beebs". That's what he called me back then. That day was the birth of the finest girls' softball team ever put together known to the town of Ottawa, Illinois and the surrounding areas. It was Laurie's and her older sister Kathy's doing, rounding up the people to create this team. At the time she and I were thirteen, the youngest players on the roster.

Laurie came from a very athletic family. She was one of six kids, second to the last in birth order; every single one of them were athletes… good ones at that. For me, all I knew was that I could catch any dodge ball thrown at me, and I was a fast runner.

Within a matter of days, the team was complete, and a coach had been selected. Naturally, it was one of my dad's friends that had been coaching little league for years. His daughter was one of the older players selected for the team, and he definitely proved his coaching skills throughout the season. When the practices began it was all about seeing who was best at playing each position. When it was my turn to test my hitting skills, I still remember the coach pitching the ball over and over, though I don't quite recall all the swinging I must have done. Finally, he walked over to me and stood behind me raising my left elbow up, telling me to keep my nose in line with my right shoulder, and to widen my stance. That day was the first day I had ever picked up a bat, and thanks to that coach I learned I could hit the ball out of the park. The year was 1977, and Santucci Shell was formed as this outrageously phenomenal softball team that went for three straight years undefeated. Some of the best memories of my life came from those years. As much as my mom wished I hadn't somehow turned into a tomboy, she never missed a game and sure was proud of me for the way I played.

Being one of the younger players I ended up playing right field. Anyone who plays baseball/softball knows that many times the right fielder is the one who will not see as much action. Because of this, when I did have a fly ball to catch, I had a tendency to make it spectacular and people marveled over my astounding catches. This behavior eventually landed me in center field. The park we played this summer league in during home games, had a large area outside the outfield perimeter on the other side of the chain link fence. People would park their cars and sit on their hoods drinking beer while watching us play. One of my fondest memories is something I will remember until the day I die. I will never forget when I chased down a ball that was hit dead center to the fence. It seemed like I was running at top speed forever until I finally reached the ball that nearly went over the fence. As the powerhouse opponent was rounding second-base on their way to third, I grabbed the ball, as I threw it aiming for home plate, the entire crowd and all my teammates watched with anticipation (definitely a slow-motion moment) as the ball sailed right into the catcher's glove as they tagged the runner out while they slid into home plate. There were two guys sitting on the hood of a car behind me, one of them yelled, "holy shit! You should be playing on the other side of the park with the boys!". I knew they were right, but they would never know just how right they would become. At that moment, I knew I had to be more than just another tomboy.

When I was around twelve my mom walked into my room and put a light blue pamphlet on my bed and walked out without a word. The pages were filled with medical drawings of the internal female organs and how and why a woman has a period every month of practically the rest of her life; it might as well be anyway. I looked through it and read the captions underneath every picture. I thought to myself this can't possibly be something that I will have to endure; somehow it will just pass me by. After all, at that very moment I had not developed breasts, I rode a dirt bike, and was mistaken for a boy fairly often.

Life was good then until the following summer. One of those days became the worst day of my life as I wiped myself after going to the bathroom, and there it was, right there on the toilet paper, bright red and screaming at me. I couldn't believe it. I didn't even know what to do. I started to cry at first realizing there was nothing I could do about this puberty thing. I certainly hated the fact that I had no control over this horrible situation. What was my mom thinking with just putting some stupid educational crap in front of me? Would this not have been the time for a quick conversation? Now I had to go and tell her what had happened as I began feeling sick to my stomach.

It was an incredibly awkward moment while she sat in the living room in one of the blue Lazy-Boy rocking recliners we had. I walked up to her with my head down, my face hidden from my big mop of curly hair, my hands on my knees standing in front of her now. She looked up at me and I said, "Mom...I started my period." "Oh, go into the linen closet and get a pad", she said. Then that was it. I went to the linen closet, the same exact place on the tiny floor inside where the box had always been, which contained something I didn't understand at the age of two while I stood with my mom in that hallway watching her get one of those horrible things called pads. They didn't even have the sticky strip on them. That is really all I remember about the whole incident when I was faced with having to get one for myself, not feeling much like a boy that day. It will always remain one of the worst days of my life. Even watching commercials for those kinds of products with my mom in the same room was very uncomfortable. I didn't hate life, or who I was, it was *what* I was.

Life is funny the way that we are conditioned; how we just seem to accept things as they are because we were told to do so. If you're a girl, you are to have crushes on boys and vice versa. Up until the age of fifteen this wasn't a problem. It's not like I could completely deny the fact that I was a girl, and up until then it wasn't so bad, with the exception of the monthly nightmare. There were still times I looked more like a boy and continued to be mistaken for one on more than one occasion. This never bothered me.

Boys liked me and I was often asked to be someone's girlfriend. I would agree just so I could wear the guy's cool ID bracelet. Those were very popular back in the late 70's and was the tell-tale sign of who you belonged to for that week. Was this only a mid western thing? I just wanted my own, but with a different name on it. The ones the girls had with their names on them were lame. They were a thin feminine version of the boys' ones.

Sometimes I would go into the local jewelry store that sold them, just to stare into the case where the ones sat intended for boys and men. I desperately wanted one for myself to wear, it didn't have to have a name on it right?

Starting high school was interesting to say the least. I was incredibly lucky to be a popular kid, and not someone who was ridiculed and teased. By now my mom and I argued over the clothes I wore, all the time. When she would take me shopping for clothes, she continued to drag me through the girls' section actually expecting me to pick out some hideous outfits. I told her I only wanted to wear Levi's and t-shirts. This really aggravated her to no end. Finding a happy medium was almost impossible. I loved my mom so very much, but I always felt as if nothing I did was ever good enough; at least according to her standards. She was one of those mothers who expected to raise perfect children. I imagine it started to become very unbearable for her, watching her daughter turn into a boy. Not only had she watched me from a window inside the house, as I jumped off wooden bike ramps built in the street; she couldn't seem to deal with me being gone all day every day during that summer down at Laurie's house playing football with the kids in her neighborhood.

I was a mere fifteen still thinking I needed to have a boyfriend since that is what everyone did. Two houses down from Laurie lived James. He was a year older than me.

His dad was a skinny guy that worked at Kroger's. He never said much, so that made being over there easy enough. James had a purple 1974 Plymouth Duster that didn't run; I guess his dad planned on fixing it up for James since he had turned sixteen. We used to sit in the back of that car in broad daylight and make out. I remember his room was at the front of the house; like a porch converted into a bedroom for him. It was long and narrow instead of wide. His twin bed was up against the common wall shared by the living room. This wall had windows with curtains, and a couch up against it on the living room side.

There were several times we would end up there, on his bed fully clothed, dry humping each other. Sex was never an option; it was just not something I could fathom for several reasons, and he was never one to push…no pun intended. With the window being right there, James' youngest brother would draw back the curtain while he sat facing the back of the couch on his knees, peeking in on us to catch a glimpse of the activity. He probably grew up with vivid memories of that, but we would have to stop and act as if nothing was going on. That was probably for the best. We were going steady, and I wore his class ring… serious stuff you know. This went on for a year and a half. We never saw each other naked. That was not an option in my mind. Aside from the fact I was young and not ready for a sexual relationship, it wouldn't be until years later that I would begin to understand my own body dysphoria issues. Rubbing clothed body parts: yes; nakedness: no. He never even asked about that.

One of those summer days, playing football with my new friends in a small grass lot on their street, James and I ended up diving for the ball at the same time from opposite sides. I slammed my face into his head. It was one of the only bloody noses I ever had; and it was a bad one. James took me back to his house, blood was everywhere. His mom took me into the kitchen to clean me up while James found me a pair of his shorts and a t-shirt to wear home. I said my goodbyes and climbed onto my blue Schwinn 10 speed bike and headed for home, through the side streets and up the steady incline of route 23.

When I came into the house, my mom was standing with her back to the upstairs kitchen sink, in front of the window facing the street, so I imagine she saw me ride up. She looked furious with her arms crossed and a crazy look on her face. I stood there with my usual white converse shoes with red stripes and white tube socks; yet missing my own clothes I was wearing when I left earlier that day. "Why are you wearing James clothes?" she asked. I explained to her what had happened during the football scrimmage. She replied, "Just go back and fuck James again", seething while she spoke. All at once I was filled with anger and pain. I stepped towards her as she was backing up against the sink now with nowhere to go. I grabbed her by her shirt and put pressure on her back as I was pushing her into the counter. "Don't you EVER say that again." I said while standing two inches in front of her face. She looked at me like I might kill her as our eyes were fixed on each other. She never said another word as I let her go and walked away. I recall wondering why she could ever have thought I was having sex. That was the only time that four letter word came out of my mother's mouth. I was not raised around cussing. Both my parents smoked, my dad drank, but neither of them cussed! Not around us kids anyway.

James took the relationship much more serious than I did. He had started mentioning marriage and I just was not there at fifteen. It wasn't long after that incident with my mom that I broke up with James since it was pointless for me to continue a relationship with someone who thought I was going to marry them. This seemed to be a common theme all too often with the boys I dated. I wasn't about to marry anyone. That was the furthest thing from my mind.

I'm not sure I can accurately explain my mother's disposition. She did the best she could raising us kids. I reminded her of that often when I reached adulthood. She placed unrealistic expectations on us as children. We are who we are, regardless of what others think. She expected her daughter to behave like a lady; not sit with spread legs like a boy. When I was six, she put me in a ballet/acrobat class. What I got out of the class was how to fall and not break bones when I played softball; and go into a tuck and roll when I threw myself off my dirt bike while popping too high of a wheelie. What she wanted, was a ballerina. During one of our arguments, over God knows what, she said to me, "I adopted a girl, not a boy." That only made me smile, because that is what I felt I was, therefore it certainly didn't hurt me.

Now, the time she hurt me the deepest, I would say since I can't seem to let it go, was when I was fifteen. I was working because I wanted to have more money than my allowance. My dad happened to own the tavern/restaurant next to the gas station, so I was able to land a dishwashing job there without having to go through the application process. When my mom's birthday was coming up that year, I saved enough to buy her something nice. I like giving unique gifts that are meaningful, so that is what I set out to do with my extra money. The most expensive shop in town was called the Deloreon Shop. It was full of beautiful, breakable things. More than likely that was the reason my mother never took us in there as little kids. I rode my bike downtown a few days before her birthday, hoping to find something really nice for her. There were so many glass cases filled with such elaborate trinkets.

Then I saw it, sitting among several Plexiglas squares set atop dark wooden bases. It was the most beautiful blue and purple butterfly I had ever seen; in fact, the only one I had ever seen. The reason being is they are a species from Peru, South America. My mom's favorite color was blue. Our front room had blue furniture and the shag carpet had blue and purple mottled through it. The gift was perfect, and it was expensive. Fifty dollars in 1980 was a lot of money to spend when you're fifteen. At the Deloreon Shop they wrapped gifts for you, making it even more beautiful to me.

I couldn't wait to give it to her to open. When the day came, it turned out to be very uneventful for my mom since my dad wasn't the best gift giver. He couldn't have used the excuse he had forgotten her birthday since their birthdays were only a week apart. I went to my room to retrieve her gift while she was in the living room dusting. "Mom, I have something for you, happy birthday." I said as I handed the gift to her. "Oh! Thank you!", she said sounding surprised. I was on the edge of my seat waiting to see her expression when she saw the beautiful creature. I watched her face as she untied the festive bow that held the lid down. She didn't have any idea in the world what she was about to find once she lifted the lid off the perfectly wrapped package. As she removed the lid all together and peered down inside, I couldn't tell whether she was surprised or shocked. She lifted the colorful insect up and said, "Wow, that's beautiful, I have never seen anything like this before." With that, I stood up to hug her and felt pretty good about my selection. She then thanked me while giving the gift placement on one of the oversized wooden octagon shaped end tables we had in the living room. That's where it would stay for several years. I really can't recall how many weeks, or possibly months, it sat there until my mother ended up in another fit of rage for some unknown reason. Over the years I have tried to recall the exchange of words but cannot. There is a very good chance it had nothing to do with me, at first. I was the one who became her sounding board and ended up hearing and witnessing the majority of her venting anger. She was a very good-hearted person, but at the same time the most bitter, grudge holding individual I had ever known. On this particular day we were alone in the living room when she started ranting and raving about how no one loves her, besides the dog, and how her birthday has been forgotten in the past. She was seething with anger and continued on about how horrible her life was. Then while I continued to stand there out of respect for her, not really wanting to hear anymore, she picked up the beautiful gift I had given her for her last birthday, and threw it across the room at me, while yelling at me what a stupid gift it was. That brought me to immediate tears. All I could do was turn and walk away.

That was forty-two years ago and I'm still not over it.

Due to my mother's behavior, I spent a lot of time outside the house and away from home when I could. Weekends consisted of me spending a lot of time on the south side of town with Kenzie. We had met in seventh grade which was called junior high back then, not middle school. She didn't like staying over at my house much because she feared my mom a little. I couldn't blame her. The fact that we were nearing sixteen came with some changes for me. Though I never had a problem finding a boyfriend, I was beginning to feel more and more out of place in the role of a girlfriend. I needed to figure out what and who I was. This was the beginning of the emerging alter ego within.

TWO

I had kissed several boys, and after all it was just a kiss. Even to the point of making out, I was never interested in doing anything other than that with any of them. It just never entered my mind. I'm positive I would not have known what to do besides kissing anyway. I remember once in sixth grade a boy attempting to describe sex; I just couldn't grasp the logistics of such an act. I pictured two people facing each other in a sitting position with legs spread, feet touching and…that was as far as I could get; I was lost. It would still be a few years before I understood how a penis goes into a vagina. In the meantime, I felt it was time to experiment a bit. In my mind I was not really a girl, and I certainly had always felt more like a boy, so why not just move on with that feeling? I shared with Kenzie how I felt on the inside. She is a very open and non-judgmental friend. I asked that she refer to me as Eric from now on. I chose that name at the time because I was a big White Sox fan and my favorite player was third baseman, Eric Soderholm. I had only been to two White Sox games with my dad. One of them, Kenzie came along too, and we both got a good number of autographs that day. I wonder what happened to those pieces of memorabilia!

The first excursion to Chicago was just me and my dad accompanied by a friend of his, and his son in 1978. This boy was the same age as me and he was both cute and popular. Though I barely recall, we had engaged in some kissing in the back of the truck, yes at the tender age of thirteen. Later this same boy would end up in my first car when I was sixteen and he became the only boy I ever started to give a blow job to. We had driven my car to what we called *the garden*, the place where I learned how to ride both a bicycle and a mini bike. An old man named Patty, who always wore a well-worn straw boater hat on his head, lived there. He walked with a wooden cane due to his right leg being almost entirely bowed out to the side. He lived in a tiny mustard yellow shack with an outhouse, no plumbing and no electricity. Attached to the house was a tiny garage that he squeezed his massive 1973 powder blue Plymouth Fury in as far as he could, leaving the back end sticking out another two feet. This property was also where both my dad and his Uncle Frank planted vegetable crops of their own every year. I became a corn shucker and green bean snapper in the summers when my dad brought home brown paper grocery bags full of his crops. There were industrial sized gates that would swing open on either side of the road going into *the garden;* large enough to drive a semi into. Patty had a dog named Rex that didn't seem to like females. It flattered me that Rex took a liking to me; that dog loved me…he ran with me and played for hours! Back to the blow job. The reason I pulled into *the garden* for any such activity was because it was a place that I felt safe, and no one would even know we were there. We never went steady; we were just there on that day seeing what either of us might get out of the afternoon of raging hormones. We chatted for a few moments before he began to unbutton and unzip his pants while sitting in the passenger seat. There were really no words, just awkward instinct as I put my hand on his penis, watching it twitch and grow. For me it was more of the fascination of the function of this organ, and this may have been when penis envy began for me. Although I don't quite remember how that escapade ended up, what I got out of it was more of an education on how a penis works.

Kenzie and I would spend the night at each other's houses frequently that summer. Now spending the night at her house was starting to take a bit of a turn. I suggested that now since I was going by a boy's name, I was going to have to start doing things that boys do; like kissing girls for instance. Kenzie had no problem with this. I can't even say that I remember the first time we kissed since it had become so often. Every time either of us would spend the night at each other's house, it happened. I recall with incredible detail of how it would go down at her house. In her bedroom she had this wooden box that looked just like a stereo speaker with a frosted piece of hard plastic covering the front. It was hooked to the stereo as an auxiliary, and it flashed different colors to the beat of the music. It was one of the coolest trendy things back then. While we lay there on her bed and watched the lights in the dimly lit room, listening to a Barry Manilow album, the intense making out would begin.

At my place we would sleep downstairs talking while watching TV, lying on the floor on several layers of sleeping bags underneath blankets that served as our sleeping quarters. I would move in for the kiss which would turn into a lengthy make out session, never anything else; just a lot of making out. It's not that we didn't have anything in common besides the fact that we both could kiss for hours, there was that other thing too...

Through enough time spent together, we realized we both were "sensitive" to those who no longer shared our time and space; at least not as we know it. We both had our stories of encounters with strange happenings in our own houses. I told her of the shadow people in my room, how sometimes one of them would sit on the edge of my bed between my feet as if they were mimicking my cat when she was not in my room. My cat would always lay between my ankles when she was in my room. I was younger when most of them would visit, and I was afraid. I never told anyone about it; figured maybe everyone had these kinds of visitors. Sometimes one of them would say my name very fast in my ear like the spirit was running right past me in the house. Kenzie had her own stories as well. I thought a Ouija board would be a good idea. I was more than ready to dive into the world of spirits. Our first incident we encountered with the board in her bedroom was intense. Whatever we had said that night in her room had conjured up several negative energies right outside of her bedroom window. She knew they were there, but I didn't believe her. She opened the curtains and yelled, "look at all of them!" I really didn't see the same things she saw, and I certainly was not afraid. To this day she describes several orb-like shapes looming outside her window with nothing but doom on their agendas. I thought Kenzie had lost her mind that summer night.

The next time she spent the night at my house, after our make out session, we went into the playroom, which by now included a ping-pong table. I loved playing ping-pong and found Kenzie to be a worthy opponent for me. After ping-pong, I wanted to give the Ouija board another try. I pulled it out and set it on the floor in front of the ever-changing light and shadows coming from the television set. "You are crazy if you think I am going to mess with that thing again", she said. "I think you are overreacting just a bit", I told her. To me, this thing was nothing more than a toy; it did say Parker Brothers on it after all. Kenzie agreed to play just one more time with me. We sat on the floor across from each other placing our fingertips on the funny shaped piece of plastic with the see thru circle in the middle. I kept trying to remember to just barely touch it in the event that it began to move on its own. The room was pretty dark, especially once we shut off the TV. With our eyes shut feeling a bit loose, and relaxed I suppose, I began to feel our hands move ever so slightly. I opened my eyes looking at Kenzie with her eyes still shut as the planchette started to pick up speed spelling out things that didn't make sense to us; at least not then. The room seemed to become darker as the board began to shake. I felt some sort of electrical surge run through my fingers. At that moment Kenzie screamed and threw the board toward me. "Get rid of it!", she yelled. By now I was freaked out while I scooped it up and ran over to the big double-sided wash sink that we had in the basement. There was a medicine cabinet on the wall above this sink where my dad shaved every morning. I looked into that mirror and thought I saw the image of a very tall dark cloaked figure. I grabbed a lighter and tried to light the board on fire. Nothing, not even a burn mark, was beginning to form as the flame licked the wood continuously. I was paralyzed with fear and figured I needed to give God a try being Catholic and all. No sooner than I said, "Our Father", the board burst into flames. I looked up at the mirror, the tall one was gone; or so I thought. I would discover several years later just how interested spirits are in the living. It seems the more complex a person's psyche is, for whatever reason, draws them in even more.

As close as Kenzie and I were, we also had our other friends and activities away from each other. Naturally, I was on the girls fast-pitch softball team in high school. I met a girl on the team that wasn't a player. She kept stats. She wanted to be involved with the team since she couldn't run. Even though we were in the same grade, I never knew her until high school. I never saw her around town before. Growing up in a town of 20,000 people you get to know a good portion of them. I even memorized several people's license plates over the years. Anyway, this girl was handicapped. She had no use of her legs but opted to hold her body weight up on crutches instead of using a wheelchair. She drove a car on her own, using metal sticks to control the pedals with one hand, while steering the non power steering wheel I might add, with her other hand. This was done by a solid plastic ball that was fastened by a bracket and screws. She spun that steering wheel effortlessly. From all her years of carrying her own weight around she was pretty damn strong. No one, boy or girl, could beat her at arm wrestling. She was a straight A student and class valedictorian the year we graduated. We got to know each other during the bus trips to our games.

The best thing about being in a sport at school is how you get to leave the class right in the middle of it without a word. You get up, give the teacher a quick look, they give you the cool nod, like saying, you're good to go on and win one for us. It was awesome every time. It was both me and Laurie leaving the same class at the same time.

During the bus rides I would sit by this girl and talk to her. I told her about my alter ego "Eric". I told her how I was a boy on the inside somehow and that was all there was to it. She agreed that I certainly acted like a boy, and even looked a little like one.

It was my junior year, and I was failing History. I hated it since it was incredibly boring to me. I didn't care at that time in my life what the hell had happened 100 years ago, though I have changed my mind on that drastically; I love history now! My history teacher was Mr. Anderson, also boring as hell. He was also the tennis coach, so he had an interest in anything pertaining to tennis. One day he announced he was passing out an article about a famous tennis player he had read about. I honestly can't remember any of his words as the sheets were passed back, and it didn't matter. When I realized what I was looking at, it was the beginning of my understanding about what was going to change my life incredibly down the road.

The article was about Dr. Richard Raskin, a professional tennis player who in 1975 underwent sex reassignment surgery out of the country. From that, emerged Renee Richards who took part in an amateur tennis competition in 1976 where it was revealed she used to be a man. This sparked a huge media frenzy if you can imagine. That led to the United States Tennis Association trying to ban her from playing in the US open in 1977 citing a so-called woman-born-woman policy. She took them to court and won the right to play. What I continue to ponder to this day, is what was Mr. Anderson's reason behind passing out the article? Somehow, I don't think he was supportive of the idea; it was 1982 after all. I felt a huge sense of relief as I learned I was not the only one who felt this way. Immediately after learning what a transsexual was, I headed straight to the school library scouring any article pertaining to the possibility that this explained my own ordeal. It was tedious work back then finding very small mentions of such a thing, especially in the Midwest. I had finally come across a man in St Louis named Dr. Packman; yes, really. I was thinking the same thing since it was my favorite game back then. I wrote down his address and tucked it away for later reference.

By the end of that school year and going into the summer before becoming a senior, I ended up spending a lot of time with the handicapped girl; her name was Diana. This was the time I became very serious about becoming the boy on the inside. I had found an ad in the back of a porno magazine for a fake penis that I could have shipped to me from a place called Van Nuys, California. I can't even recall receiving the box, but I'm sure I kept watch diligently until its arrival, that would not have been a good thing for my mom to retrieve from the mail box.

What I do remember is putting it in my pants and looking at myself in the mirror thinking all was right with me for that moment. I couldn't leave it in my pants walking around the house; it was way too noticeable since it was always in the erect position. Even tucking it underneath was not going to hide the entire thing. I hid it in the upstairs bathroom next to my bedroom under the sink. Every morning before school I would slip it in my pants and be sure my shirt was covering it. I was so obsessed with having it with me, I began to play softball with it there as well, and ended up bruising myself with that thing from all the diving and sliding I did during a game. Don't ask me how I got it to stay in place well enough with all that kind of movement, the strangest memories become nothing but blurs.

I had met a girl in Art class that was a freshman when I was a junior. Margot was hilarious and we had many conversations while doing our projects. It didn't take long before Eric had emerged in the friendship. Margot would find herself flirting with me, yet if I was not portraying Eric at the time, I would get annoyed by the advances. This confused her somewhat, but she was very open minded and continued to be a good friend. I invited her to spend the night at my house one summer weekend and she accepted. Of course, since she was there with my family, we would have gone to bed with me in the female persona. Once we were alone in the basement, I made my move, and we began making out. I asked her to hang on a minute, while I went to get to get my spare part. I came back and when we resumed our activities, I put her hand in my nether region and she was perplexed. She said she wanted my female persona back. I immediately went and put my part away and we didn't talk about it again…at least not for 35 more years.

I had convinced Diana while we were on one of the bus rides to a game that what was in my pants was real and I would grab her hand and try to make her touch it. I knew she wouldn't but she sure was a blast, so I ended up going over to her house pretty often. We would hang out and listen to Air Supply in her room and talk for hours. One of those days I was sitting at the typewriter in her room when a friend of hers had come by who lived just two doors down. When she came in, Diana introduced us. "Eric, this is Jana, Jana, Eric." This cute girl slipped right behind me, bent down and put her arm around my neck like a little hug as if she already knew me. I certainly wasn't going to stop her. I was instantly attracted to her and I think she knew that. The fact that this little alter ego thing was taking effect on other people was perfect for me. Even though some of the people around me accepted this name alteration as something normal, it certainly was not going to be that simple with everyone else, like these girls' parents for instance. Especially when Diana's mother had found the diary Diana was keeping hidden in her room. She wrote of a boy named Eric she was spending a whole lot of time with. I never saw what was written, but it had to be more than just being friends with him; since her parents flipped out and assumed Diana was secretly seeing some terrible boy that was taking advantage of their daughter. Now when they learned this boy was me, things got way worse, I'm sure you can imagine. Diana called me at home and told me her parents demanded I come over there ASAP with my mother. Hell no, I wasn't going to bring her! She doesn't and cannot know anything about my alter ego. I called my Aunt Eleanor, my dad's sister, who was the polar opposite of my mother. I was having a complete meltdown over the whole thing, so she agreed to meet me at Diana's house. I waited for my aunt outside in the street because I felt they thought I was a deviant. I did not dare set foot on the property. When she arrived, we walked up to the door together. I felt like throwing up. Both Diana's parents met us at the door with incredibly stern looks on their faces. We walked to the kitchen where Diana was sitting at the head of the table. My hands were dripping with sweat, again I wanted to puke. Diana's mom began by outlining my masquerade, and just how horrible it was. "Do you have any idea what *she* has done to my daughter?" she blurted out to my aunt. To this day I wonder what really was written in that little book. I never even kissed her let alone anything else. Was it wishful thinking on Diana's end? I will never know.

My aunt, being a very open-minded person, the exact reason I brought her along instead of my mom, tried to explain my behavior with the definition of a transgender person since she felt that might be the probability. I remember thinking how incredibly intuitive she was. None of that mattered to them, they would hear none of such a thing and I was booted and banned from that house forever.

My immediate attraction to Jana, along with her obvious one to me, made me begin spending every day at her house, and becoming quite close to her parents. These people lived in a very simple tiny house, and Jana's parents were very simple dressers. Her dad wore industrial work pants and a white t-shirt every day. While her mom was the more puzzling one to me with her Lee jeans, and depending on the weather it was just a t-shirt or a sweatshirt, just plain and simple, very different from my mom, who on the other hand, was constantly in style within her age range of a little above average clothing for this small town. One reason I'm sure for their dressed down attire was they just didn't have very much. Her dad, who slightly reminded me of John Cougar Mellencamp, worked on restoring cars but I don't think he was paid for that very often.

I still remember when he had brought home a 1967 Pontiac Firebird with its original factory metallic green paint, with rusted quarter panels. Its interior was not too bad besides needing a good cleaning since it was white. I don't know what he paid for it, and it didn't matter because by the time he was done with it, he had restored it to show room quality and gave it to Jana when she turned sixteen. That was quite the first car let me tell you! I watched him turn that car into a dream. Everything was stock; he just fixed it all and gave it a new coat of candy apple red paint.

To make things even more interesting, I had actually known Jana's brother Brandon from back when I was in junior high. He was a year ahead of me though he was a little slow; he had the body of an athlete which always intrigued me since I was already obsessed with the male physique. After attending a roller-skating party, we had been picked up by Blaine's mom. Blaine was one of our mutual friends that I had known since fifth grade at St. Columba. On that ride home, Brandon and I ended up rolling around in the back of the van for a quick make out session. Blaine's mom didn't mind what we were doing while she was driving. Maybe she was getting off on it, who knows. So, there I was, no more than fourteen with my hands down this boy's pants grabbing at a penis I only wish I had. She had dropped us both off at my house, and when we got there, I ordered him into our garage back behind our big maroon colored 1974 Oldsmobile 98, and told him to take his pants down. He did as I said. I pulled on that penis for quite some time which must not have been going as well for him since he asked me if I was done yet. Done touching it was all he wondered. He was not allowed to touch me and I think he was fine with that. I was just completely curious about this piece of flesh that could change size so quickly when persuaded to do so. I didn't know anything about turning someone on and neither did he at such a young age. Thinking back now, I'm sure he was probably super nervous thinking someone could walk in on us. Good point, but my mind was too fascinated with what I was holding in my hand; wishing I had one of my own.

Even though that had been all of three years previous, I was spending time at his house trying to get with his sister, it was a bit awkward. Jana and I spent every day together. She called me Eric, and she saw me as a boy. Every day, every chance we could go to her room and shut the door we did. Even if it was only for a few minutes it was filled with passion as I would push her up against the wall and kiss her long while we started a heavy make out session. Looking back, I cannot believe the risk we took as her bedroom door did not even lock. Even though there were times I put my hand underneath her clothes, she was not allowed to do the same because I couldn't allow her to know my secret.

When she would spend the night at my house, we slept in my room, on my waterbed. All I wanted to do was hold her all night after we made out for at least an hour, along with clothed humping with my erect penis friend in my pants. When she was ready for sex, I was her first, with the use of my spare part. I was seventeen and I was in love with a girl and even though in my mind I was a boy, that really can only take you so far. Although this was only a charade, it was very real to me.

THREE

*T*hat very summer I fell in love was the same summer I went to Europe. Kenzie called me and asked me if I might want to go, to be a part of a group called ALSG: American Leadership Study Group. This was an organization that offered discounted educational tours abroad. I initially said no. At seventeen, I had no urge to travel to a place so far away and this also meant being away from Jana for an entire month. Kenzie could have cared less for my undying love for some girl, and figured it would be worth our while to take on such a venture. My mom also thought it would be a good opportunity as well. After some coaxing on Kenzie's side, I agreed. Now this meant attending weekly meetings with other kids we didn't know from our town. There were two high schools in Ottawa, Ottawa High and Marquette. Students from both schools were attending. These meetings were held at the home of Mrs. Schneider, the woman who would be our chaperone. Mrs. Schneider was very fun as I recall. Her daughter, Jan, was our age, so naturally she came along.

We would visit Barcelona and Madrid in Spain; Florence, Rome, and Venice in Italy; Monaco; Nice, France; Lucerne, Switzerland; and London, England before returning back to the United States. My mom actually paid for the trip with money she made baking cakes. She took every opportunity to remind me of all she did for me throughout my life. It's not that I am not appreciative of all she did for me, yet when she was upset with me, I got the list of significant things she had done for me. The trip was something like three thousand dollars back in 1982. That covered airfare, all the hotel accommodations, and a daily breakfast that consisted of endless pastries.

My most vivid memory of the trip was the flight from Chicago to Madrid, Spain. The planes that fly internationally are the enormous 747's with two levels connected by a spiral staircase. One of the things I will never forget was flying from darkness to light, watching it change as quickly as the plane moved through the clouds; it was very surreal for sure. We would travel between countries by bus. This was similar to traveling from state to state in the United States. For example, in a passenger car it is around six and a half hours from Barcelona, Spain to Nice, France. A bit longer on a bus full of teenagers.

A good majority of the trip is now just snippets in my mind having its highs and lows. I knew one day I would appreciate the fact that I had the opportunity to go whereas then, it didn't matter that much. The mind of a teenager can be a thankless thing. I didn't care for Barcelona. The outdoor markets have slabs of meat hanging on hooks with flies attaching themselves to it. A vendor asks you as you walk by if you would like a sandwich. Are you kidding me?

The hotel we stayed in had a disco tech below and as much as I liked the song" Tainted Love" by Soft Cell, it was insane to hear it over and over and over again when one is trying to recuperate from jet lag. Those Spanish people love to party well into the next day. I remember when we were in Italy, Kenzie was tired of hearing how much I missed Jana, while I was foolishly spending money calling her in the United States, which I find crazy now. In order to keep my mind off of Jana, Kenzie figured she would throw herself down on the bed, pull her shirt up exposing her washboard abs tanned by the summer sun, and pull me on top of her all-in-one motion. It did work; I did kiss her, but nothing else. This was in the middle of the day, I'm not sure where everyone else was. We were, after all, on a group trip. We were interrupted by a frantic knock on the door propelling me off of Kenzie, and on to the floor. After pushing myself up, I walked the few steps it took to get to the door. Opening it, there stood one of our roommates, who thankfully forgot her room key. She began babbling about how Kenzie and I were absent for the current headcount as we were all about to converge on

The Sistine Chapel right there in Vatican City! With that said, both Kenzie and I grabbed our canvas ALSG shoulder bags, as Karen swiped her key from the nightstand she had left behind. "Come on! we have to hurry up you guys, everyone is in the lobby waiting for us!" said Karen, as we bounded down the white marble steps looking over the massive railing, there they all were, all of them, some spilling out the front doors to the street, waiting for us.

As the droves of teen-aged kids continued to move like cattle to the exit, I could see our local little group waiting, while the circle of chaperones talked. I caught Mrs. Schneider's eye of half frustration, although even when frustrated, she always had a lighthearted, carefree way about her. When we reached our group, Mrs. Schneider winked, and hit me with her warm smile letting me know she wasn't mad at all. I was relieved, that's for sure. We proceeded to fall in line with the massive crowd heading to one of the most famous places in the world. Vatican City, though surrounded by Rome is the world's smallest, fully independent nation-state, having everything to do with the Roman Catholic Church.

Walking the streets of Rome is very different than that of anywhere in the United States. With all the massive fountains serving as traffic circles and scads of local people riding past on Vespa's beeping their horns at you, hoping you will get out of their way.

Anywhere there were crosswalks, the metal street signs had stick figures running, not walking! I didn't have a vision in mind of what to expect prior to approaching St. Peter's Basilica. It was enormous and utterly breathtaking! The Sistine Chapel inside Saint Peter's Basilica was a marvel to say the least; pictures do not do it justice! Once we walked through the doors, it was like being transported to a massive castle finding yourself surrounded by marble and stone. There is much pomp and circumstance to many other things other than God Himself. That seems a bit problematic for sure, nonetheless beauty beyond the imagination. The Sistine Chapel attracts thousands of people a year to experience the astounding fresco paintings on the ceiling, painted by Michael Angelo between 1508 to 1512. His final task was to sketch on the ceiling, then paint three- hundred figures illustrating the pre-history of salvation, moving through human's time spent on earth, before the coming of Christ. There is everything from the creation of Adam, to the fall of man, angels and demons, clouds and chaos, and God himself creating the cosmos from day one of the seven. Both breathtaking and awe-struck are most appropriate words to describe the ceiling while looking up. They all seem to be looking back down. Even at seventeen, it was something that I felt fortunate to have the opportunity to experience, along with sitting on the concrete spectator steps inside the Colosseum in Rome; yet another deeply moving experience.

Our next destination was Nice, France. Shockingly, many of the women do not wear the tops of their swimsuits on the beach, and the men all wear Speedos, very different from here. If that wasn't enough, Kenzie and I spotted a sex shop while strolling down the shop lined street near the beach. In France, we were able to walk right in and begin to browse without someone asking about our age. It was time for a new penis, and I couldn't believe the selection and the fact that underage kids were just welcome to browse. How wonderful it was to just pick one out and not have to wait for it to be delivered.

On our way out of the store two young French guys spotted us coming out of such an establishment, and started walking towards us pointing at their own personal regions while nodding their heads up and down. We looked at each other and just took off running as they followed. We ended up losing them ducking into an alley that merged into a side street paved of cobblestone. There, we joined up with the rest of the group as we spotted them browsing along the pop-up vendors on either side of the street.

That month went pretty fast, the only regret I have to this very day, was when we were in Paris. We had already walked a significant amount that day. We all stopped to rest awhile next to the river Seine, that flows below the Eiffel Tower. When everyone was getting up to walk over to the tower I didn't budge. "Are you not coming?" Kenzie asked. "No, I can see it from here." Idiot is the only word that comes to mind of my younger self that day.

When we returned from Europe, I was twenty pounds lighter since I refused to eat a good majority of what was offered outside of Italy. To this day I am still a pretty picky eater.

I had missed Jana incredibly and spent the rest of the summer with her at my side. We went back and forth with our relationship. She would stop seeing me to date other guys. Once just to be with her, like a love-sick puppy, I would agree to pair up with a guy that was a friend of the guy she was going out with that night.

Graduation day was freedom. That's what it felt like anyway. There are photos of me and Stacey together on that day in our red caps and gowns. We had become close our senior year, and her mom was super nice to me, liking me enough to allow me to move to their back porch the summer of 1983. Me, my dog Teric, and my waterbed. The time spent with Stacey did evolve into a physical relationship. She too saw me as a boy, though she knew that wasn't exactly true. Her mother never knew, and to this day I'm not sure if she ever did find out. If so, it would not have come from Stacey. That fall I moved with her to Peoria, Illinois very briefly where she attended school at St. Francis Hospital, which is where I was born, where my birth mother had given me up. I definitely did not want to move back to my parents' house, so when Stacey moved to Peoria, I felt that was my only option at the time. Stacey was studying to become a histotechnologist (tissue preparation examiner). She tried to get into the archived birth records to see if she could find my birth mom, but with no luck. Little did I know at the time, my birth mother was looking for me as well.

I grew antsy in Peoria and announced I was going to return home to Ottawa. Arriving in Ottawa, I found an apartment. The first call I made was to Jana. I invited her over and she brought a pizza. We talked and caught up. We made out a bit. She used the restroom and left for the evening. Then the day came when I went to see her at her work, and she refused to speak to me. She wouldn't even look at me. I knew we had our problems, but didn't see this coming. I left and drove home to my apartment. I wasn't home for five minutes and I heard pounding on my door. I answered it to Jana's mom standing there just staring at me. She looked very upset but did not speak. I asked her in, then shut the door. As soon as we entered the front room area, she just started pushing me without saying any words. I let her do that a few times until I was mad enough to push back, forcing her to fall into my little Christmas tree. Then she began yelling, "You have torn my family in half! You took my daughter's innocence away from her! She can never get that back you piece of shit!" "Never, ever go near her or my house again!" "Look, she did love me, and I can prove it!", I yelled. While she sat there motionless on the floor, her face beet red from anger, I went to the bedroom closet where all the love letters from her to me were in a cigar box up on the shelf. I slid the door to one side and went to grab the box but it was missing. I suspect Jana took them the last time she had visited me. Jana's mom picked herself up off the floor and I never saw her again.

I had come to a point where I really needed to find a job. I checked the want-ads and saw an opportunity that was too good to pass up, selling vacuums for big commissions. The day that I interviewed for this job; well really just agreeing to push their product, I met a girl named Alexis. I was binding my chest at this point, but still had to go by the female name to get a job. I told her my name was Eric, I could pass for a guy by binding my chest. That was the most hated part of my body, the telltale sign when you can't decide if you are looking at a man or a woman. Along with the impressive looking package in my pants, how could I lose? I got her phone number right before she was called in for her interview. She was called prior to me so she didn't hear me called in by my real name. I ended up taking the job; I know, it's lame and they always promise you big money on sales. I sold a few, one being to my mother, and it was big money, just very short lived.

I invited Alexis to my place, which consisted of a small living room, kitchen, tiny bathroom, and one bedroom. There was a door off the bedroom to the outside yard for Teric and her wading pool. I actually kept my dirt bike in the bedroom since I had no garage. We had dinner, talked about music and movies. She told me her father had transferred with Borg Warner in West Virginia; that's how they ended up in Ottawa. After talking we moved to the bedroom. She wasted no time taking off her clothes. I, on the other hand, had to think quick on my feet. I told her it must be completely dark, and I preferred not to be touched. She was certainly confused. I left my shirt on, took off my pants leaving my underwear on with my French souvenir tucked away ready to go. I would grasp what I so wished was real and slowly guide it in. It was intense and passionate. It was not long before she moved in with me. This girl was a sex machine, sometimes three times a night. The story I had come up with to explain the rules I imposed on intimacy was that although I was a guy, there was a defect at birth that had to be fixed surgically.

The first thing was going to have to be making a trip to speak with Dr. Packman in St Louis. I called and made the appointment, knowing he was the only possible link to beginning to deal with my situation; or so I thought. I can't recall the price tag on one appointment with him, but I do remember it wasn't cheap. He is a psychiatrist, and back then there was no one else to see about being transgender, a term not even known at that time, at least in a small town. This was the Midwest. Not many people knew you could have a sex change. You would think there would have been an awareness in the medical field, especially by a professional that claimed to specialize in gender issues. This would not be the case when I walked through his office door, dressed as a fine young man, I might add.

His office was massive with green plush carpet, a huge mahogany desk and very expensive leather furniture. I sat down in front of his desk, and immediately noticed the entire wall behind him was bookshelves. I had never seen such a large bookcase outside of a library. I was a bit nervous not knowing what to expect. When I explained to him how I felt like a man trapped in a woman's body he said. "Just admit you're gay". I couldn't believe it. This is not what I just drove over four hours for. This man knew nothing about gender dysphoria or simply didn't care. I left his office broken, and pretty much still feel the same way about it to this day. We were supposed to stay at the Clarion Hotel that night, but I was so upset we just drove back home. I couldn't even tell Alexis why I was so upset since the truth was a very big secret.

We never discussed it, and then one day I came home; she had cleaned out the place, took most everything I had and left me the animals. She moved in with some guy she met at work. I can only speculate that she started to actually think through the rules I had laid out in the beginning of our physical relationship. So instead of trying to talk to me about any of it, she bailed. I know I wouldn't have been able to come clean at that time anyway, it was too hard to face; the truth I mean. It wouldn't be until almost 40 years later that I connected with her on social media, that I would begin to understand the mental affect my manipulative behavior had on those I had deceived. It was never my intention to hurt anybody; for the sake of self-preservation, I was trying to make myself who it was I saw in my mind. When I was fully clothed with my chest bound and my spare part in tow, the illusion in the mirror was my truth.

Alexis had moved to Ottawa the year prior, so she had no idea of my true identity or my family background. Diana knew my real name prior to the induction of "Eric". She saw me as a guy regardless of my born gender. Jana went to the other high school in town.

Both these girls' parents knew who my dad and my grandfather were; they were both pillars of the community. I was quite proud of that, but now was not the time to boast. Then there was Stacey, she too, knew my true identity, but bought into my story as well; they all did. In my mind it was easier to create this male alter ego instead of ever trying to explain that I was this term called transsexual that I myself was just beginning to understand. I recall my explanation for my reason for changing my demeanor was more like a dual personality kind of a thing.

Prior to puberty, although there were markers that indicated I had male tendencies, I complied with societal norms. Once puberty hit, the maleness inside needed an outlet. The only way it made sense in my head was to have two completely different personalities. I did have boyfriends while in the female persona, yet the male persona was stronger. I never considered myself a lesbian as I was male to the females I was with. I do know that I had told the girls I was with that there had been some kind of strange mistake prior to my birth, and it was going to take me some time to get it fixed. It certainly was not a mistake; God doesn't make them. I also knew it would cost money I didn't have. I couldn't think that far into my future to know if I ever would.

I had to find another place to live. My dad's cousin had passed, and she left him executor of her will. Therefore, he oversaw the house she had just died in. He told me I could live there if I wanted while all the legalities were being settled. When the estate was settled, my parents decided to buy the house after living in the house I grew up in for twenty years. I was a bit surprised by that, my mom said she cried all the way down the hill when they moved.

I had been working at Handy Foods for a while now, which was one of three locations owned by a family I grew up knowing. I went to elementary school at St. Columba with the owner's kids. I worked in the kitchen and after some time, I asked people to just call me "M". I simply couldn't tolerate the female name anymore. It is so odd remembering how well the people there took to this request; at least the ones working with me. The owners were friends with my parents; I cant imagine that not being discussed behind closed doors.

A new girl started working there in the deli along with Pat, who was a really nice older lady. "Pat, who is the new girl?", I asked. "Jim's girlfriend, Robin", she said. Jim also worked there with me in the kitchen. What I knew at that point and time was that I wanted her to be mine, so I walked over to her behind the deli counter and simply said, "Robin? call me M", while I stuck my hand out waiting for her to put her hand in mine. She was confused by both who and what I was, but seemed interested as she offered her hand saying, "very nice to meet you...M." As late afternoon became almost evening, I was finding it hard to not take notice every time Robin would walk through the double swinging doors to the kitchen to grab a to-go order for a customer. I was pretty sure she was doing the same thing, since I would catch her looking back at me several times. Jim was oblivious to the situation.

Since it was Robin's first day, she was only there a few hours. After I clocked out and made my way back through the kitchen and out the double doors, Robin's white satin windbreaker and perfectly fitted Levi's caught my eye as she walked down the aisle heading to the front of the store. I picked up my pace to catch up to her and said, "Hey, do you want to order some food to go, and come over to my place?" "Sure", she replied. "Great, just give me ten minutes to grab us a couple of tenderloins and fries, sound good?" "Oh yes, I love tenderloins!" She seemed very excited, and I was very surprised when she accepted my invitation. I explained to her on the two-minute drive how and why I was staying in an unfurnished house, and that I had plans to move to Southern California soon. She proceeded to tell me that she had been born at Camp Pendleton Marine Corps Base, which is in Southern California. I found that a bit interesting. Robin was from the next town over and even though we went to the same high school, I didn't know her. She was a year behind me in school, so as far as I knew, she never saw me before we met at Handy Foods.

She was very shy but was very drawn to me. I could feel it. We sat at the kitchen table that was still there, thankfully. We sat next to each other talking about this and that while getting through supper. When I started to get up from my chair and grab our to-go boxes off the table, she ran her hand up my thigh letting me know we were on the same page for what comes next. I pretended it didn't effect me, but my heart was pounding faster as I threw the trash in the can.

I knew she was right behind me, so I took her hand and lead her to the sunken room that had a wooden pocket door, with carved out Japanese-like shapes. I had my Pioneer stereo system set up in there, so I figured what better room to take her into, turn some music on and lay some blankets on the floor. I then lit a candle to pair with the perfect music station to set the mood, barely registering "Dreams" by Fleetwood Mac before Robin's hands slide around my waist and pulled me back towards the blankets. The familiar anxiety pushed to my throat as her hands start to drift upwards, so I quickly caught them and spun us around. "I don't like my chest to be touched", I said. She shrugged, "Ok", as her hands settled back on my waist, and she stepped so close that we were pressed into each other now. She didn't say anything else, just pulled our hips together.

I couldn't believe this was all happening so fast. It was hot and steamy. She pulled back for a moment, I felt like she was going to tell me that this is a mistake; that she is James' girl, and this isn't right, that maybe she should leave. Instead, she tore her shirt off, and we were back at it again. "Just let me take care of you tonight." I told her. The pure physical attraction was intense, again I spoke of the rules while I was helping her slide off her Levi's. She never uttered a word; she just pushed herself up to kiss me. While the candle provided a pleasant glow, it wasn't enough to see anything in detail as we were entangled in the throes of passion. Then we laid there and talked until we were out of things to say. She never asked me to explain why my shirt and underwear need to remain on. No one ever did.

We moved the blankets into the master bedroom. In the pitch blackness I brought up my plans to move to California again, though I still didn't know what city, just that I knew I was going. I never really had any actual plan; I just knew I had to go. That night while we both were asleep; my eyes flew wide open in the darkness to see a light bulb falling towards my face which shattered before it hit me. I could hear the song "Blue Bayou" playing down the hall and thought, how in the hell did my stereo come on? I got up and to go shut it off but when I reached the pocket door, it had stopped as if it was never playing at all. That was my most intense paranormal experience to date, and yet there was still so much more I would encounter.

The next morning, as I blinked my eyes open to the sunlight streaming in through the faded blinds, there was a knock on the door. Robin rolled over to look right at me, "someone is here." Another more frantic knock followed, forcing me to pop right up to answer the door. While rounding the corner to the kitchen there was more intense knocking. When I reached the door to open it, I could see it was Jim standing there looking panic-stricken. "Jim? What's going on? Are you crying?" His glassy blue eyes stared at me, "Well…um…is my girlfriend Robin here?" "Who told you she might be?", I answered. "Her mom said she didn't come home last night when I called for her." "Ok, but how did she…" At this point Robin was behind me, and spoke past me saying, "Jim, I don't need you looking out for me, in fact, I'm breaking up with you to go to California with…him." She said as she now stepped in front of me with a jutted hip and her arms crossed. "Robin, please don't leave, I love you." He said as he burst into full-blown tears sending fat drops down his cheeks. "Please baby, please don't do this!" This scene was becoming quite uncomfortable, I was embarrassed for him. "I'm staying here Jim."

I felt bad for him, yet if she had gone with him, I would have been fine with that too. I think he really did love her, and I'm not sure why she picked me, not even knowing me, and then add in all my personal physical hands-off rules. Once Jim reached his home, he called me pleading with me to make her go back to him, maybe I should have. It was not my decision, it was Robin's.

One afternoon while Robin was taking a bath, Alexis showed up at the door a little tipsy.

I opened the door and she came right in, pushed me up against the wall and started kissing me. Maybe the new guy couldn't satisfy her? I went along with it, grabbed her hand and took her downstairs to where my waterbed was now set up. We jumped in and screwed. You may be wondering how could I have done that to Robin? Good question. I think about that and realize how much I didn't care about anyone but myself. That was the last time I ever saw Alexis, except from a distance once, years later while I was visiting, she had a small son by then.

Stacey had returned from Peoria and was back at home with her mom, which was down the street from me now. Her dad had died just a couple of years before when we were still in school. I watched as he flat lined on the table while peering through the small window of the room at the hospital. She was seeing a guy named Mark, and it turned out that his brother lived in a place called Riverside, California; so that became my destination.

Prior to us leaving, I was foolish enough to dabble in the investment of a rock of cocaine. I gave this guy I knew from school one thousand dollars, and he was supposed to double my money; I lost every dime. What an idiot maneuver. That was most of my traveling money, but Stacey came through for me letting me borrow most of what I lost. My dad bought me a different car since the one I had would not have made the trip. He never thought I was really going to go, he laughed when I told him. He was of a generation that was born, lived, and died in the same town.

The first car he ever bought me was a 1975 Buick Special; an odd light green color with gold stripes on the sides. I would have five cars in between the one he bought me to drive to California, which was a 1978 white Ford LTD with red leather-like interior. I got bored mostly, and forty-one years later, I estimate I have owned well over forty cars. I just have to take the time again to write them all down.

Before leaving Illinois for California, I had to legally change my name. This required a petition to the court and going before a judge as to why. Also, it had to be published in a newspaper within the county it was filed. Because I knew how much this was going to hurt my parents if they were to read it, I chose a paper outside of Ottawa. I was changing my whole name; first, middle and last. The newspaper it was published in was almost twenty-five minutes away, but naturally many people knew my parents branching out away from Ottawa. A random woman from that town called my mom wanting to know what was going on. I don't know how good of friends they were, but I didn't hear the end of that for years.

Next, I had to go to the local DMV to change my name on my license with my court papers in hand. There I was greeted by Mrs. Johnson, the mother of June, a girl I hung out with in elementary school. They lived in the next subdivision on the other side of the ravine. I'm sure that was the topic at dinner that night. She did her job and gave me a new license that read Marco Anthony Roselli. It was great besides for the gender being "F".

As clever as I was, I decided to modify the "F" to an "M". It seemed harmless enough. By law you cannot change the gender of any legal document without having proof of sex reassignment surgery. I didn't care about that; all I knew is I wasn't going to move to another state with a male name and an "F" gender on my license.

Thinking back now, I cringe at the impulsivity to just pack up a car, filled to the brim with whatever personal possessions one feels compelled to bring on a 1,980-mile journey across the country. Let's not forget the girl I barely knew and a Samoyed dog. It was quite a shot in the dark, even back then. But that is what I had to do to get away from the place where many people knew my secret. I couldn't continue to live a life that I considered a lie on the inside; and certainly not there, in my little home town. I had no idea at the time what really lied ahead and at twenty-one, I figured things could only get better. As the day drew near for our departure into the unknown, the reality hit what I had to endure. I couldn't ignore what I really was; physically, anyway. The masquerade would have to continue indefinitely; I really had no plan.

FOUR

(MAY 1986)

*M*y nightly routine after showering was binding my chest as tight as I could with the six- inch bandage that needed to be so tight, there were times it constricted my breathing.

I had to sleep with it on so Robin would not know of what laid beneath my t- shirt. I knew this charade could only go on for so long if I were going to be living with this girl, so I had to come up with some story as why I had to hide my deformities; that is what they were to me anyway. I was lucky enough to pass as a guy even with a smooth face. The younger, the more reason a guy may lack facial hair. I was twenty-one but looked sixteen.

In the early morning hours of the next day, Robin and I were doing all the last-minute preparations for our incredibly exciting trip to California. Gathering up all we had planned to take; saving room for Teric in the back seat was a feat in itself. Over breakfast before our departure, I asked Robin if she was sure she wanted to come along with me, and why? After all, we had really only just met. "Of Corse I want to go with you Marco, why would you even ask?" "What if you don't like it out there?" I asked. "I will be with you, and that is all that matters". "Alright then, let's hit the road".

With the big atlas mapped out and ready to go, I was prepared to drive seventeen hours straight through to Wheat Ridge, Colorado where there was a Ramada Inn waiting with our reservation. We both had said our goodbyes to our parents the night before. My mom was beyond trying to understand what I was, and what I thought I was going to accomplish by moving so far away. Driving through the town took all of ten minutes to get over to Interstate 80 and head west; this was both exciting and a bit sad. This place that I grew up in served me well, but I knew I could not stay. As we turned onto the interstate, I slipped in one of Elton John's less popular cassette tapes, *The Fox*, as it played the song *Chloe*, and we rode away from home. It was about nine hours into straight driving before I felt as if I needed some kind of push to continue on. This was long before energy drinks or shots; which I care for neither. I prefer shots of flavored espresso myself; although that wasn't even a thing then. I recall buying some kind of pick me up pill at a gas station while re-fueling, I'm sure similar to speed since it did take me the eight additional hours it took to reach our Colorado destination, this was our halfway point. Once there, in Wheat Ridge, we had to sneak Teric into the room; thank God she wasn't a barker. We ordered room service, I remember I had steak, then we crashed until the next morning. As we moved through the Rocky Mountains for the first time in our lives it was a bit unnerving when it seemed the car might roll backwards on the incredibly steep incline; that's how I remember it anyway. As the day turned into night again, all of what seemed as endless miles, are now just a blur being so many years ago. When the city lights of Riverside had come into view from the top of the Cajon Pass at 2:00am, I was completely mesmerized by such a site, knowing that was the place I was going to now live. That was my first experience of a culture shock moment, along with just barely being able to see lines of palm trees in the dimmest of light bouncing off on coming cars from the other side of the mountain pass.

Not being familiar with the area we ended up exiting at University Ave where there seemed to be several motels from which to choose. The streets were rather bare being the very early hours of the morning, which was a plus since I hadn't realized I had blown through a red light. Not five minutes into Riverside and there is already flashing red lights in my rear view. "This is great, damn it!" I had said, as Robin looked behind us. I pulled over the big white boat of a car and waited for the officer to approach the window. I pushed the power button to lower the window; my hands were sweating now. "Yes officer?" I had said. "You do know you drove right through that red light behind you?" she said. A female officer: this was a first for me. Imagine that, California is very different from the get-go, I was thinking. "I really didn't see it since I was looking for a place to stay, we just got into town", I had told her. "I will need your driver's license and registration please." "Sure thing". I reached into my wallet and pulled out my license as Robin was fumbling for the registration in the glove box.

I handed her the license and registration, and she went back to her squad car. When she came back to my car, she clicked on her very large flashlight and looked at my ID and asked, "Are you contemplating a sex change?" *Holy crap, how did she know?* (I'm sure when she ran my license). Then she said, "I see you have manipulated the gender; do you know that's illegal?" "No, I never gave that a thought, and yes to your initial question." "I'm going to let it slide, welcome to California", she said. With a sigh of relief, I said, "Thank you."

We spent the night is some little dive that we found. In the morning I went out and bought a newspaper out of a dispenser on the sidewalk out front. I scoured rentals looking for a place to live. I made phone calls from the room until I found something promising. We ended up driving over to a place on Arlington Ave across from Rohr Aircraft industries. It was a complex of studio apartments. The first clue I had there was going to be a language barrier problem, was when we pulled into the parking spots that were labeled "VISTOR". Are they kidding me? Why can this person not spell? I wondered. We walked into the tiny office and were greeted by a nice middle aged Hispanic woman. I explained to her that we had just arrived to town and needed a place assuring her we would both have jobs within a week. "As long as you give me two months' rent, then that will be fine." She had said. "That's great, thank you." I said as I handed her 600.00 cash making us new tenants of a 350 square foot studio with a tiny kitchen and bath.

Robin's mom ironically had a friend that lived right down the street in a small neighborhood from where we now lived. She gave us some kind of wave less waterbed, soft-sided mattress. That was fortunate since we didn't have any furniture. We had acquired a framed picture to put over the bed, and a small T.V. on a little stand in the corner of the opposite side of the room. It was home for now.

The first order of business was getting jobs. We continued to look for want ads in the newspaper the first few days and both of us went for interviews at Pizza Hut. With my experience at Bianchi's pizza back home made me a shoe in for a line cook and oven worker as well. Back in my days with Bianchi's I learned to become quite the showman with the pizza crust tossing. The building in which Bianchi's existed, used to be an old ice cream parlor many years ago. The ceiling stretches twenty feet; it has a functioning National cash register in the front along with an old black barber's chair you can sit in.

And, the best thing to me was the jukebox that played the 45's. I had talked the owner into letting me update some of the musical selections at the time; 1982 that was. I guess my contributions are still there, I can only hope. The cool thing was we had an eject button under the make table if we were really tired of hearing some of the lame music that was in there. It is located very close to Ottawa High School so after football games the place was packed, even with all its extensive seating. There were kids waiting out the door on nights like that for a seat. I would give them a show with the tossing of the dough, with all that head room, it looked pretty impressive. This was before he had conveyor belt ovens, only deck ovens. This is the only way to become a true pizza maker if you ask me. There are four doors to an oven in which the pizzas are put in and have to be watched and rotated out and the next ones come in, having up to six pizzas per oven door, you have to know when to rotate, pop bubbles, and pull them out. When those ovens are full with one person manning it, it becomes an art. This art made me the main oven worker at Pizza Hut at the time.

Robin was hired as a waitress. We both had jobs by the fifth day of living in California. Times sure have changed since then as far as job hunting goes. The uniform for Pizza Hut then consisted of brown pants that were a poly blend kind of fabric and a short-sleeved button-down shirt. The guy's pants had a zipper, but not the girls. During my interview with the manager of the store I was sweating slightly over the fact that my license was in an altered state. What will I tell her,

I wondered, if she saw its mild alteration? With luck on my side, she didn't notice it. The other factor about my license was the photo. I was twenty-one, but no one ever believed it. I was certainly never offended by this, hoping that my baby face would serve me well into my forties. My God that seemed so far away then. I knew full well that the other reason I looked sixteen was my lack of facial hair…zero. Since this was prior to me injecting testosterone into my body I had to improvise. People were going to notice at some point that I never even had one strand of hair on my face, no signs of remote stubble by any means. I did have perfect skin, just too smooth.

I found myself relegated to looking in costume shops for some kind of substance I could apply to my upper lip to suggest the shadow of a moustache. I really hadn't given the whole five o'clock shadow thing a thought up to that point, and now it was just another detail of being male I had to try to mimic, not knowing how to realistically pull it off. As I browsed the isles in one of those pop-up Halloween stores, I came across this dark brown kind of oily substance in a little jar that from a distance, passed as the beginnings of facial hair. Close up though, was another story.

I always felt I needed to be on guard at all times, even more so the closer in physical proximity anyone was to me. There was a girl at work, her name was Kari and clearly was one to notice details, in this case, the lack thereof. I had noticed her one day looking a little too hard at my upper lip as she reached out for it, I blurted out in panic, "Don't touch it!" Jerking her hand back she said, "I wouldn't think of it." No one else there had ever thought anything about me was odd. I had my chest flattened down, and a *noticeable*package in my pants along with the bluest eyes, and long lashes to boot. I must not forget my dark curly hair girls always wanted to touch.

I could have slept with any girl I wanted, but my secret was a big one and had to remain hidden. I had the apparent pleasure of meeting Lori; who was a common customer who became obsessed with my eyes. She started to bring friends of hers in just to look at them to marvel at the color. "Marco, come over here." She would say as she came trouncing through the door of Pizza Hut with a female friend or two. "Are his eyes not the most beautiful blue you have ever seen?" They would agree with her as it boosted my ego every time. She was a good friend of a guy that worked there along side of me, Matt. He was the reason she was hanging out there on the weekends. Now he had a girlfriend named Hope, who was very pretty. His female tendencies at times, perplexed me, I still wonder to this day if he is possibly gay.

Mine and Robin's relationship was alright I guess, but I certainly was not in love with her. At that time, I really would not have known what love is. She, on the other hand, was very possessive over me. She would get mad when Hope would purposely lean into me pressing her boobs against my back, when she would put tickets up from behind me while I was on the make table busy making pizzas. Naturally, I didn't mind, and apparently Matt never noticed. Another person I met there was Darla, she wasn't there every night like I was. Robin hadn't met her yet since we hadn't been there that long. I used to make fun of her for what I called her sensible shoes. They reminded me of some orthopedic numbers that only old people wear. We got along very well and she ended up inviting me and Robin out to her and her husband's place for a barbeque.

When I got home that night, I started out just telling Robin about Darla's and my conversation and she became immediately suspicious. "Does she want to fuck you already?", she snapped. "Are you serious? She's married, and invited both of us!" This behavior was becoming constant, and something I had a hard time dealing with. "Well, when are we going then?" she asked all of a sudden calmly. "Tomorrow afternoon at one." I replied.

The one thing that Robin wanted most was a baby, something I hadn't given much thought to. Let's see, now how will I accomplish that I had wondered. First of all I had to come up with a story as to why someone else's sperm was going to be necessary for the child to be "normal". At this point she did not know I could not father a child. I told her this crazy story that my "stuff" was contaminated by some less than friendly spirit force and it was going to take the sperm of another person to counter act the "bad seed". Crazy as hell, but either she bought it, or mentally ignored it, not wanting to question me.

I ran an ad in the paper for a handyman. When the guy called, I simply told him he had to come over to our place and jerk off into a plastic cup, and I would pay him 40 bucks. I was relieved the first call was the taker, since that was not something I wanted to continue to repeat. I don't remember his name; he was short like me but had blonde hair and blue eyes. When the day came for him to come by since it was an ovulation day, he was handed a plastic cup and pointed to the bathroom doorway. I guess it was about ten minutes or so and he stepped out with his sample. I paid him his 40 dollars on his way out. The next step was the turkey baster. This was the first failed attempt for a pregnancy to take place.

Darla's husband Walt, had turned out to be a grill master. Outside of general conversation the topic of religion had come up somehow. Both Darla and I came from Catholic backgrounds, and Walt from Jehovah Witness. These two people got married to get out of each other's parents' homes. Now, the strangest thing about Walt to me was that his sister was married to the brother of Tom who was dating Stacey back home, the one telling me before I had left, that his brother lived in Riverside, which is not a small town. How incredibly weird is that? What are the odds? They told us they went to a church in Riverside that was non-denominational. That kind of thing was very new to me. They invited us to go naturally, and when I heard the description of the whereabouts of the building, I knew exactly what they were talking about. "We go past there every day on our way home." I had said. I wondered what it was, and a church was not one of my guesses since there was no steeple.

Walking into this place was very different than any Catholic church for sure. It was more like an auditorium, walking first through one of four sets of double doors to the entrance of the foyer, on to three more sets of double doors serving as the entrance to the sanctuary. When I pulled open a door I was blasted with rock like music, a far cry from the haunting pipe organ music so often played in Catholic churches around the world.

The seating seemed endless, with what I noted was the absence of kneelers, that I came to learn are not necessary for the worship of God. No ornate décor or statues of anyone, anywhere. No stained glass, no even a cross. I learned the reasons for the absence of such things, none of them are to be prayed to or worshiped. I definitely got that, never understanding confessing sins to a priest, rather than taking the direct line to God himself. The direct worship of Mary and praying to saints is the furthest away from God.

I rather enjoyed the music and came to understand there really is such a thing as Christian rock. We continued to attend this mega church on a regular basis for the most part, and it was there that the bible came alive and relatable, very different from the Catholic way.

This is where I began to understand the reality of being able to have an actual relationship with Jesus, not just hearing the same stories about him, year after year.

I know for a fact that my being in the right place at the right time brought me there. It was the first stepping stone. Faith is, well, just that. I certainly did have it in God, but no direction in obtaining much else. I spent years chasing after my own true self making many mistakes along the way. I was a very tortured soul both on the inside and out.

This had become the very reason I had left Ottawa seeking a broader horizon in Southern California. I was one who could not envision spending the rest of my life in a small town, though it certainly was a great place to grow up back then. The goals I had set upon myself were not attainable, I had to go to become who I had be.

FIVE

As obsessive as Robin was about me, I was about to find out that when she was sought after by another, she did not hesitate to concur on some level. A guy name Doug began working at Pizza Hut after we had been there a couple of months. He was immediately drawn to both Robin and me. He was near me at my every move it seemed, always asking me questions and wanting my input, as if I was some kind of idol to him.

That summer while Kenzie was on break from school, she decided to take a trip to visit me. She flew into Ontario, California (not Canada), that at the time was much smaller than it is now, but also much closer than having to drive to Los Angeles to pick her up, not to mention evading the horrific traffic found moving to and from the greater Los Angeles area. Before the Ontario expansion, passengers would disembark down a ladder on the tarmac, and we were able to meet them right at the gate. I spotted her in an instance descending the steps. She looked good coming down that is for sure, and whatever kind of odd attraction we did have toward each other, it was never meant to go beyond a physical fling every now and again. As she came towards me with one bag slung over her shoulder, I grabbed the other case in her hand while I grabbed her and hugged her tight. "Damn, it's so good to see you." I said to her. "Yeah, it is." She was always short with the words if it involved emotion. "Where's Robin?" She asked. "At work, we can drive over there now if you are hungry." "I am, nothing on the plane interested me much." She answered.

I had taken the next five days off to spend with her and planned on having a good time. As we drove away from Ontario off to Riverside, we talked about what she wanted to do while in California. "Well first of all, I bought us front row seats to David Bowie for tomorrow night." "What?!" "How much did that cost you?" "200 bucks a piece through a scalper". "Are you kidding me!?" I found that almost unbelievable to say the least. "I guess he's alright" I said. "Just alright?!" she shouted. "Are you crazy!?" She said while smacking me extremely hard on the arm. "He's a god!" She insisted. "What do you think of all the palm trees?" I decided to ask her. "Very tropical like". She answered. "To me they are the epitome of a beach paradise, even though the streets are lined with them." I had told her.

As we pulled into Pizza Hut's parking lot it was apparent that they were swamped, making it hard to find a place to park. When we walked through the door, Robin happened to be swiftly moving through the dining room attempting to service two tables at once. She had inadvertently made eye contact with me when noticing I was not alone as we stood behind the *please wait to be seated* sign. Once she had a moment, she came over to bring us to a table slamming the menus down just a little bit. "Hello Robin." "Hey Kenzie." At that awkward moment I looked up to see Doug making a beeline to our table, I'm sure the suspense was killing him as to who this girl was that had come in with me. "Marco, my man!" "Hey Doug, this is my friend Kenzie from Illinois, we met in seventh grade, and are still friends eight years later. "Nice to meet you Kenzie, maybe we can all do something together while you are here, that would be great!" "Yeah, great." Kenzie responded unenthusiastically. "Doug can you please go back to what you were doing so I can take their order?? Robin said, clearly irritated by Doug's presence. "Fine!" he said while putting both his hands up and in front of him, turning and walking away. "Ok, we're just going to split a pan pizza with ham and cheese." I said to Robin. "Are you now?" "Um, yes, we are… and two Pepsis as well." By then she had turned away from us not even saying a word.

After we were full, we left and headed to my studio apartment to hang out and catch up. We were both laying on the bed, there was no other place to sit, not even a bar stool that would go in conjunction with the three-foot counter opposite the kitchen sink and tiny stove. The entrances to these studios consisted of a sliding glass door without curtains. Anyone passing by could take a peek if they were so inclined. As Kenzie had burst out laughing at something I had said, the door slides open just to bounce back from being slammed into the frame on the other end, with Robin crossing the threshold, "Oh no, she's not staying here! Where in the hell is she supposed to sleep!? Cause it sure is not in bed with us!" "Why do you have to completely flip out?!" Kenzie is scrambling behind me trying to reach the door as quickly as she can, bag in hand. "Why did you bring her here is a better question?!" Robin said to me in her attempt to deflect her behavior. "Because I live here, I thought maybe we could figure something out on the sleeping thing!" I said as I walked out the door.

Kenzie was propped up against my car with her arms folded watching the traffic breeze by. "Kenzie, I'm sorry this has happened. I really never had any kind of plan for your sleeping arrangements." "It's ok, I just need a place to sleep for a few days." We pulled up to the most decent motel on Tyler Ave and got her checked in. The room was upstairs with a fabulous view of the street. As we put her bags down, she moved towards the bed grabbing my hand and pulling me down with her. She had already had her shirt rolled up exposing her flat tan abdomen. She knew that would make me lay there with her. As usual we started to make out most intensely; it's just what we did. After a few minutes she pulled away from me and said, "Right now, as you are I am attracted to you, but once you actually change your body parts I won't be any more." "This would be the reason we don't go any further for me anyway because I need to be a man physically in order to be comfortable with a woman touching me."

If anyone understood me, it was Kenzie. She didn't put labels on people, she just went with what felt right. I must admit that makes things easier, but the majority of society does not follow that idea. She is attracted to mainly woman, and only effeminate men. She does not label herself as lesbian or bi sexual. She did marry a man many years later after this visit; in order to have a family I suppose, though she swore she would never give birth. She is one of the most trustworthy and loyal people I have ever known, which is why we have remained friends for the last forty-four years. As much as she would rather be sleeping with a woman every night, she stands by her man who fathered her children.

The next night she and I saw David Bowie in Los Angeles during his "Serious Moonlight" tour. The day after that was all about site seeing, and Doug had decided he would come along. Naturally he thought he was going to somehow get into Kenzie's pants by the end of the day, he had no idea who he was dealing with. Like most visitors to Southern California, we wanted to check out some of the stars' homes, for Kenzie, particularly Cary Grant's. She was a huge fan of him as well. We decided we would just do the driving on our own and not be tied down to a tour bus. We went by several homes including Lucille Ball's which has been destroyed, by the way, and a different home now stands. It has been said that after the demolition of her home, the one she shared with Desi Arnaz and raised their children; a female spirit resembling Lucy has been seen there just standing in the rubble.

As we approached the walled area of Mr. Grant's fine spread, we decided to park the car on the side of the road and walk to the perimeter of the property to see if we might get a better look. I was not too keen on the idea. I'm not one for invasion of privacy on any level. However, as a stroke of luck for Kenzie, we all witnessed Cary in a white robe and his twenty something year old daughter come out of the house and on to the pool deck.

Now I saw Kenzie trying to scale the concrete wall, and Doug yelling at them trying to get their attention. I was mortified. I told them both they needed to calm down, and we should probably go. That was not going to be the case. They decided we should camp out awhile at the grand black iron gate until it opened for Cary to leave his fabulous fortress. After some time, I certainly could not believe my eyes as the gates started to slowly swing out on both sides while the little black Volkswagen Cabriolet with tinted windows waited patiently for clearance to proceed.

Like the fools they were that day, they flagged the unsuspecting motorist down to stop. I really was surprised when the car actually did stop. They both ran over while I stayed back. The tinted glass slid down to reveal Cary's daughter. "Where you headed?" asked Doug. "To the Red Onion," she replied, as she began to drive away. I hadn't lived in California long enough yet to know what that was but assumed it must be some kind of cool hang out for the children of stars. I would later learn it was a Mexican restaurant with a dance club in the basement that had a few locations around greater Los Angeles. Doug was getting on my last nerve that night, when he asked me if he could crash at our place. "We don't have anything for you to sleep on, you know that." "That's ok, look what I found while walking the wall." He said, while proudly holding up an obviously discarded piece of metal patio furniture with woven orange plastic designed to hold weight. "So, this is your traveling bed?" "Yeah, why not?" Why I couldn't tell him no is beyond me.

On the drive back from Los Angeles, I dropped Kenzie off at her motel, then Doug and I made our way to my place. "Exactly where do you live Doug?" I realized I knew nothing about him other than we worked in the same building. "I stay here and there, not really a secured address." "So, your homeless?" "I don't call it that..." "But you are, and your not staying here." "Just tonight man, ok?" Doug said, as we pulled into the parking lot. After Doug had pulled his plastic patio lounger from the back seat, while we walked up the concreate steps to the second floor, he just kept talking about how great it was that we were friends. I really wasn't feeling the same way was my thought as I unlocked our highly secure sliding glass door. While we were moving across the threshold Doug ends up slamming his lounge chair into the door frame, waking Robin. "What's going on?" She asked. "Doug is spending the night." "Hey Robin! Doug pipes in as he arranges his lounge chair into a corner. "Hello Doug." She said sleepily while I interjected, "Alright, well I'm going to take a shower, I'm taking Kenzie to the airport in the morning."

With the sun up, I was awake finding Robin asleep next to me, and Doug in his fancy lounge chair coiled up due to lack of a blanket I imagine. After getting myself dressed, I grabbed my wallet, keys, and a piece of peanut butter toast I began to eat as I headed out the door. The motel was just ten minutes away, and the Ontario airport twenty. Not too bad when compared to LAX. When I arrived at the door of the motel room, Kenzie was sitting on the bed waiting for me, bags in hand. "I'm really sorry about Robin's behavior." "It's fine, seeing Cary Grant in his robe was well worth the trip." "And David Bowie?" I asked. "Gorgeous as usual." Was her reply.

When I returned home, I found Doug still there standing outside the door propping himself on the railing as he watched me come up the stairs. "What's up Doug?" "Man, if Robin was my girl, the things I would do to her with my tongue…" "What? Why would you even say that man?" He had his keys in his hand, and for whatever reason he was just standing there daydreaming before I even walked up the steps. After such a bizarre statement, it made me wonder what has already happened between the two of them this morning when I was gone. I just went into my place as he walked down the stairs leaving his piece of patio furniture behind. Was he high? I didn't know much about that behavior at the time, so it is certainly a possibility.

We stayed in the studio under a year, then started looking for something a little bigger, but in Riverside that was going to be more money. We went to Moreno Valley to look at a place I found in the newspaper with the rent being similar to what we were paying for the studio. It was literally right off of the 60 freeway that I now consider pretty ghetto, and was a terrible mistake I would realize, due to the noise of the constant moving traffic. The woman who ran the place was very nice, her name was Kim, she had a son around ten or so and a woman at least ten years younger dressed in fatigues often stayed with her. She was stationed at March Air Force Base. From the moment I saw her it was clear to me they were lesbians.

The vacant unit Kim showed us was next to hers, a one bedroom one bath; at least it was a bit bigger than the studio, so we decided to take it. We certainly didn't have much stuff to move, but with having to transport the small couch and dining table along with chairs that I bought through an add, I had to solicit Doug's help. He had access to a small trailer he could hook to his car. We hadn't seen each other outside of work since the trip to Hollywood, so I had asked him there at work if he could pick those items up for me. He agreed which was a relief, sparing me from having to rent a pick-up myself. Both Robin and I were outside getting things out of our cars when Doug pulled up with the trailer. "Hey man, I really appreciate you going to get those things for me." "Never a problem Marco, is it cool if I stay on your couch a few days now that you have one?" What was I supposed to say? "Sure buddy." Is what I did say while we were carrying the couch in together.

We still spent most our time in Riverside since that is where we worked, and I personally liked the city better than that of Moreno Valley. I became obsessed with the thoughts of where to find information, or a lead to any articles on sex reassignment surgery. I had no idea even where to start or how it worked. I spent hours in the Riverside library and finally in a medical journal I came across a place in Palo Alto called Gender Dysphoria Inc. I wrote the address and phone number down, and went home and called immediately. The woman on the line was very pleasant and helpful. She took my address down and said she would send me out the forms I needed to complete along with a mental assessment that was imperative prior to even getting an appointment with these people. Understandable since there have been people over time that have gone through having surgeries and then regretting it later on. I can't even imagine that myself.

Within a week of Doug's extended stay with us, he informed me that he had decided to shack up with a woman named Ellie, who lived on the other side of our building. She was at least ten years older than him. This was a good turn of events to say the least, or so I thought. Now that he had a woman to screw, I didn't see him for a few weeks until the day he gave me a call. "Hello?" "Marco, this is Doug, can you come over here for a few? I have something for you." "Sure, I'll be right over." I hung up and made my way over to Ellie's place. I knocked on the door then heard him say, "Come in." I opened the door that swung to the right, at the same moment Doug's right black booted foot hit my face three times in less than two seconds. I fell backwards to the floor, he rolled me to my stomach then came behind me, wrapped his forearm around my neck then pulled me to my knees choking me while screaming at me; "Why did you turn me in?! Now they will deport me back to Canada you motherfucker!!" pulling his arm tighter and tighter around my neck with every word that fell out of his mouth. Ellie then came into the room though I couldn't see her I heard her say, "Doug! Let him go, or I'll call the police." With that, he let his arm loose as I fell forward, my face hitting the floor. The last thing I saw was Ellie's feet before I blacked out. I don't know how long I was out for as I tried to pull myself up from the floor, my lip stuck to carpet fibers from blood. I could hear Robin outside talking as I crawled to the door. Doug was nowhere to be found, Ellie was telling Robin what had happened not understanding it anymore than I did. I knew nothing about his supposed alien status…nothing.

I stood up, with my mouth pounding as I pushed open the screen door to the outside. Both women staring at me in silence as I walked past them. "I should go help him clean up his face." Robin said to Ellie, as she followed me back to our place, into the bathroom trying to help clean my wounds with a wet cloth. "How are you?" "How do I look!? I snapped back. "Sorry, I'm just trying to help." "Are you? Really? Do you have any idea why that might have happened?" "Why would you even ask me that Marco?" "Never mind." I replied.

Word had gotten around about Lori's obsession with my blue eyes at work, right in to Robin's ear. That evening at home she brought it up and went nuts. "Why does every girl want you?!" "Every girl? What the hell do you expect me to do?" I asked. She then proceeded to come at me full force in the small kitchen grabbing my chest above the ace bandage line twisting my skin seething while she just kept twisting. "Damn it that hurts!" while I pulled her hands off me and then shoved her up against the counter hard. She fell to the floor saying she needed to get away from me. "Good! then go! I'll buy your ticket to fly back home!" She was completely nuts! I slept on the couch that night, and the next morning I went to a travel agency to buy a one-way ticket for Robin back to Illinois.

Now I was alone and liked it. As soon as Lori knew that Robin was gone, she showed up at my door. I let her in naturally, we started to talk, she was funny and pretty, though slightly overweight. I told her Robin was driving me nuts and I didn't know at that point if she was coming back. I had gone to use the bathroom, and when I opened the door to come out, she was standing right there. She pushed me back inside and pinned me to the wall planting her lips hard on mine. I pushed her off me, telling her I wasn't interested in her in that way, which made her mad, making that the last time I ever saw her.

During the time Robin was gone I received my paperwork from Palo Alto. It was a very thick stuffed business size envelope, engulfing the entire insides of the mailbox. I rushed back inside the apartment and tore it open reading over its contents feverishly. After answering a barrage of questions, the answers needed to meet criteria such as:

- Long standing and strong identification with the opposite gender

- Long standing discomfort about the sex assigned or a sense of incongruity in the gender assigned role of that sex

- Significant clinical discomfort or impairment at work, social situations and or important life areas.

I was confident in meeting the guidelines set forth, knowing I began to identify as more male as early as ten, but tried to urinate standing up at six. My preference of GI Joe and Big Jim dolls over Barbie was clear, though they were useful as girlfriends or wives of the guy dolls I so treasured. The funny thing is my mom had no problem buying me what was considered boy's toys more than likely thinking it was only a phase, but that was just the beginning.

By the time I was twelve I was riding a BMX bike, jumping off ramps in the street and living for the Sundays my dad took us kids to a place called Consumers to ride our dirt bikes. This place was on the opposite side of the Illinois River off of De Bennett Rd that runs between Ottawa and Utica. It was full of dirt trails with both big and small jumps, created over time by others. You could ride for at least two miles before running into this big open area of clay. It went on forever it seemed with its hardened cracks baked in from the constant summer sun, the terrain looked like one great big giant puzzle! My dad trusted my riding skills to let me venture out alone, having the best times going off the same jump over and over again hoping to get up just a little bit higher in the air the next time. There was this one kid that came along one Sunday with his dad, a very longtime friend of my dad's. My dad called him Swampy, so we did too. His son was around ten or so then, riding his Honda 90 trail bike, that I thought looked ridiculous since the placement of the gas tank is under the seat. They just didn't look cool enough to me. He was riding at top speed on a trail, lost control and flung off the bike into a tree branch that opened up his leg a mile wide. It was pretty bad, and worse, there was no getting an ambulance back into the area. His dad took his 4x4 up into the trails and loaded the kid on the back of the truck to get him to the hospital. He ended up with over 300 stitches.

The water you would find back within Consumers was as beautiful as a tropical beach. We found out some years later, the reason it looked that way was due to being toxic. I never did jump in, but I saw someone else swim in there. Animals born in and around this area were missing limbs at birth. Not good.

The fact that I could hardly stand the naked reflection of myself in front of my very large bedroom mirror was a problem. Puberty is a very bad thing for a transgendered person. The misconceptions about transgendered people are mostly out of ignorance alone. A transvestite is certainly nothing even close, though there are people that think they are one in the same. Transvestites are generally heterosexual men, who for whatever reason like to dress in women's clothing, sometimes just women's lingerie under a three-piece suit. If these are not gay men or men who want to become women, why do they feel this need? I have no idea.

The worst misconception to me is the belief that a female to male transsexual was a lesbian first, before deciding to get a sex change. As true as this is many times it is not always the case. I, for one, not ever, even for a minute, identified as a lesbian; it just never entered my mind. I understand why a girl going into their teens and being attracted to girls would find it logical that they must be gay. If only it were always that simple.

Obviously, that was Dr. Packman's only view back in 1984. Even after telling my mother of how I felt, she called my Aunt Eleanor asking her, "Is she a Lebanese?" My aunt responded with, "The term is lesbian, and no I don't think that is what she is." My mother wanted nothing more to do with any explanations. Shortly after that, Aunt Eleanor gave me a book to read, and to this day I can't even recall the cover, let alone the title. What I do know now is my mom had found it, wherever it was. I must have been hiding it. She took it on a very rainy day, tossed it into her car and did a drive by in front of my aunt's house and flung it out the car window landing in a puddle on the driveway. I really can picture her face frozen in a look of anger and disgust, wondering what her sister-in-law was thinking giving me such horrible information. I never even knew that happened until years after my mother's death.

Now this is my moment to clarify to all of you who care or are just plain curious, so imagine yourself looking in a mirror naked or not, but truly worse naked. You despise your own body, but not because you're too fat or too thin. Those things you can change with will power and diligence. In fact, you might very well have a fantastic body, according to someone else was looking at you, admiring your physique. Not to you though, because that still doesn't matter since your mind is trapped in the opposite gender with which you identify. No matter how much you wish for it to be what it is you feel, you cannot change it on your own. Your life slowly becomes misery on the inside, and it might take a good part of your life to change it. Wasted time is precious. This is what I learned way too many years, and mistakes later. Though much more content these days, the climb was steep, and it's still not over. Maybe it never will be.

SIX

I had finished and put my application to The Gender Dysphoria Clinic back in the mail to return all in the same day I had received it. Mail could not move fast enough for them to receive my paperwork. Little did I know then how computer technology would change our lives forever for those after me, allowing them to just send theirs with the touch of a keystroke.

My landlord Kim came knocking on my door asking why she hadn't seen Robin lately. I told her she had flown back home for awhile, making note out loud that my neck was sore. "Guess I slept on it wrong." I had said. "Let me rub it for you." she answered.

"That's alright, Ill be fine." I tried to tell her but she insisted. "Lay on the floor, I have magic hands just for this kind of thing." I reluctantly laid on the floor feeling very awkward in doing so. After she was done with my neck, she moved down my back, making it obvious she was shifting the mood to a more sensual one. "Well, that's good, thanks, I feel better already." I told her. Then she stopped and looked at me, "Is Robin coming back?" "I don't know, and I really don't care." I answered. "You know, your hands are rather small." She blurted out. At this point I knew she was on to me. She knew I was not really a guy. "Ok, so what is your point?" I inquired. "You can come over anytime you want for a body rub of any kind." She never did say anything about what she suspected about my true identity, but she knew. That was the reason for her attraction to me. Did she think I was a lesbian? If that were the case,

I certainly would not have gone to the trouble to hide my true physical body parts I so deeply despised. Maybe since she did know she figured I would sleep with her since it wouldn't matter that I was a woman underneath the clothes. That is what she wanted after all. That only pissed me off that someone saw through it.

It would still be a while before any testosterone would course through my body, so for now other than my name change it was purely a charade. Kim left without another word. With Robin gone I spent more time with some of the people we had met through work.

She ended up being gone for a month but came back wanting to try to work our relationship out. By now we had both moved on to a different place of employment, a place called Starcrest. It is a warehouse that barely paid minimum wage. It had a clerical department, where Robin worked in data entry, and I naturally in the warehouse where I met Ted.

We got along pretty well, Robin and I had been to his place and met his wife and daughter, who was two at the time. One night Ted and I drove to the beach, I felt we were good enough friends, so I decided to share my identity with him; just feeling the need to talk about it after what happened with Kim. We sat on a ledge not far from the water and I just began to tell him. "Ted, have you ever heard of a transsexual?" "No, I don't think so" he replied. "Well, the thing is….". "Is what?" he asked. "That is what I am". "What does that mean?" Now he was curious. "I was born with a mind of a boy and the body of a girl, but never felt like one ever. I have changed my name legally to what you know it is now; even my last name to spare my parents." By this time, we were walking along the shore, and he was not saying a word. I broke the silence with, "I'm going to have a sex change when I get the money, but I'm just getting started with the steps that need to be taken to get to that point.". "Show me", he insisted. "What?" I really was hoping he wasn't serious. "Unbutton your shirt so I can see." All I wore was button down shirts so attention wouldn't be drawn to the lines created by the ace bandage that dug into by sides, constricting my breathing at times. I decided to do as he asked thinking that he just needed clarification to understand. As I began slowly and nervously unbuttoning one button at a time, his eyes fixed to my chest like he was waiting for a jack in the box to pop.

After removing that shirt, I still had a half shirt that I had cut that way so I wouldn't be quite as hot, and it was extra masking of the problem. I wore that half gray shirt underneath every shirt, everyday.

Did people not wonder why? As flattened out as my chest was from the binding, in low lighting you couldn't tell there was anything there. That was the whole purpose, especially when getting intimate with someone. I then lifted the half shirt to reveal the smashed down beyond belief breasts. He still said nothing. I imagine he was in shock, or maybe felt betrayed? I don't really know, after that, things began to take a turn for the worst.

Things went back to normal with us having sex nearly every night, thrusting in her the seven-inch dildo with its carved in veins mocking a rock- hard erection that never quit. Between all the in and out motion and the constant rubbing the fake penis was doing on my oversized "part" (I refuse to use the word to describe it) that is what brought me to orgasm. No touching me, ever.

Over the next week or so I noticed that Robin was on the phone very often with both Ted and his wife. One evening after she hung up, she said that Ted was coming over; something about my car she had said. When I heard the knock on the door, I went to open it, knowing it was Ted, but before I could get a word out, his booted foot came up hitting me square in the mouth causing splitting pain to reverberate through my skull, spinning me around. I staggered back, but regained my footing then out of reaction I took a swing at him. He blocked it, and spun around from the other side of me now, kicking me a second time in the face, knocking me to the ground this time. All I could see was blood on the floor as I lifted my head watching him fly over to the kitchen where Robin was, standing watching it all. He went to grab her, "Come on! You need to get away from this freak! We can leave together, the two of us up to San Jose." After hearing what he had said to her, I said "NO!" In a horrible sounding, blood gurgling voice. I then went over toward them trying to pull her away from him. He just looked at me dumbfounded, "Just go Ted, that was a little too much!" Robin said. With that, he was gone as quick as he came. Trying to process it, all I wondered was were they planning to get out of here together all along? Was Ted leaving his wife and daughter for Robin?

SEVEN

One bloody face for sure, boots will do that. Maybe out of guilt Robin had followed me into the bathroom trying to help me clean up my wounded mouth and eye. "Maybe you can try telling me what that was all about?" I said to her. "Ted told me what you had done at the beach." "He doesn't understand, and neither do I. You told me it was something you were born with." "It is!" I shouted, and I'm going to get it fixed one day, but let's talk about what the hell just happened here!" "Ted was afraid for me, calling you a freak." Yeah, I caught that, is that what you think I am?" "I really don't know what to think Marco, I don't even know what your name was before you changed it." "It's not important, why did he come here tonight? What was his purpose?" "He came here to take me from you." "Have you screwed him?" "Just one time." She said with her head looking down at the bathroom floor. "He doesn't love his wife, he loves me." "Really?" "When did this happen?" I asked. "Right before I left for Illinois." "When you were freaking out about girls flirting with me, yet you were screwing Ted!?" Marco, why is your dick always hard?" Don't ask me that kind of shit!"

"I never thought he would hurt you like that; I am sorry." "Bullshit! I see a pattern, don't you? Not one, but two guys have beat the shit out of me because of you." This explains Doug's behavior as well. You screwed him as well, you told him you don't understand what I am, so he tries to kill me." "No, I never..." "Liar!" "I want to be with you, but I just don't understand who or what you are." "I told you, I am a guy, just not in the regular sense, but one day no one will ever question it." "Robin, just marry me" I said with blood dripping off my lip, but clearly an insane moment for me. "Really?" are you serious?" She said out of complete shock. "Yes, let's go tonight to Vegas." "She threw her arms around my neck, kissed my cheek, and said "let's go!" She said as we grabbed a few things for the night and ran to the car. *Why are we doing this?* I was already wondering.

We drove the four hours until we hit the strip, and decided to stop at the Imperial Palace. We crashed that night, and woke up the next morning to see about getting a marriage license at the court house. There was a whole bunch of people there for the same reason.

One added feature to getting married in Las Vegas is most of the Hotels furnish a limo to take you to the courthouse. I never thought for one minute that anyone there would have thought of me as anything other than a man. I signed away the paperwork as the groom. After that, we went to the nearest little chapel around the first corner, signed in and waited in line. We both looked sharp enough for a walk on wedding. We were married in five minutes.

We both pretended to be happy; we went back to the hotel to change into jeans again before going down to the sea of people we would encounter in the casinos. The phone rang, which surprised me, maybe it's the front desk I thought. "Hello?" "You better get the hell out of there now before I find you, I know where you are." Then *click*. I had absolutely no idea who that was, for sure. It could have been either one of *them*. I never told Robin about it, and spent the entire night watching my back in case someone was going to try to stab me. We spent that night there, had some wild sex, and went home the next morning. I survived, no one killed me.

It took several weeks for me to receive the phone call I was waiting for. The voice on the other end was that of a woman sounding to be in her early thirties telling me she had reviewed my paperwork I had submitted to the Gender Dysphoria Program. She explained that they had expanded their criteria and were not accepting many patients at this time due to elevated rates of patients winding up with severe mental issues if they were not a viable candidate for such a major life change. She continued by telling me that I fit all the criteria set forth, so the next step would be making an appointment for me to go meet with her for an evaluation. She mentioned that after the initial evaluation we would discuss starting me on hormone therapy. This was great news, but the bad news was I would have to put off going for awhile. It was always about the money, or lack thereof.

We needed to move to get away from this place, and these people we had been having contact with as far as I was concerned. During the discussion with Robin in regard to moving again she said, "Let's go to Oceanside." I did like the idea of being near the ocean. My mind was so twisted then with what seemed like no way out.

Driving out toward the ocean in the summer is always best because you can feel the temperature go down as you get closer. Like every town, it had its good and not so good neighborhoods. We unfortunately ended up on the down side of this one with no furniture, no T.V., and completely flea infested. This would be a short stay, I felt as if we were fugitives. We would steal food from the grocery store; well Robin would while I was off buying a pack of gum or something. I went looking for work right away and ended up at a big car lot in Carlsbad. I worked on the lot washing and, best of all, gassing up all the used cars. I always loved it when a Corvette trade would come in. Who trades in a Corvette? A new family man; perhaps in need of more than two seats? We were barely surviving on what money we were making. After bombing the place to irradicate the fleas we ended up renting furniture, to make it like home for the meantime.

Robin had announced that a friend of hers from back home was going to fly out to see her. "Who?" I asked. "A guy named Jake I went to school with." "When will he be here?" "He is in the air now; I will be leaving soon to pick him up at the Ontario airport." "Do you want me to go with you?" I really did wonder if she wanted me to. "Sure." Is all she said, but I feel she would rather have said no. On the way to the airport, she didn't have much to say, and I couldn't quite place her mood. Our recent marriage was feeling pointless to say the least. As we stood in the breeze way off the tarmac watching the plane taxi in from Chicago, I noticed Robin seemed antsy. Like a dog longing for the return of their master. *Why did I even come?* At least the sun was down now bringing the summer temperatures plummeting. California lacks humidity with such sparse rainfall, so it cools off a lot quicker than Illinois. I had to smile when Robin began waving frantically at the clean-cut, dark-haired boy. I can always spot a Midwesterner. As they walked up together, we were introduced. "Jake, this is Marco, Marco, Jake." I shook his hand as I led them towards the short walk to the car. They were very much in a conversation of their own, whatever. On the drive back to Oceanside I felt somewhat like a chauffeur.

When we reached our new destination of living quarters, I told them I was going to take a shower and get to bed, having to work in the morning. "Nice meeting you" Jake had called out as I left the room. The next morning, they were up before me, and I couldn't recall if Robin had come to bed. "Good morning, Marco" Jake said while he was eating some toast. He was such a friendly guy. "Good morning" I replied. I too had grabbed some toast, and flew out the door. After getting all the way to my car I realized I had leftovers I needed to take with me if I wanted to eat lunch. I turned back, climbed the steps to our apartment and quickly turned the knob pushing the door wide open. With nothing but shock on both their faces while in each other's arms on the floor, panting from the recent groping session I had interrupted, they could say nothing. I just backed out and shut the door. I sat on the steps right outside the apartment door, wondering what in the hell was happening, again.

EIGHT

*T*hey both came busting out the door together attempting to apologize for their behavior. "Do either of you think I care?" I had asked them. "What I do want to know is why all the games?" Looking at Robin for the moment I said "Why did you even come back?

You could have stayed back there with lover boy here and not continued to complicate things." "I don't know why I just didn't stay; I still wanted to be near you, I cant really explain it." "Then why is *he* here?" "I came for her myself." Jake piped in. "I love her, and thought I could talk her into coming back with me today." "Well you two do whatever you want; I'm packing up my stuff and heading back home for awhile." I left them standing there as I continued down the steps to get to the job I would only have for a few more days.

"Jake, I can't go back with you, I just can't." "Robin, you said yourself that Marco really isn't a normal man, why then do you continue to stay with him?" "I don't know, I just keep hoping it will all make sense someday?" "I need to get you to the airport very soon, so maybe you should get your things together." After dropping off who could have been her new relationship, Robin had come back to find me packing boxes in my car. One of the coolest cars I had ever had, but not legally owned, since I just never did the title paperwork. Idiot is the only word that enters my mind about that. It was a 1972 Pontiac Firebird Formula 400, with a Hurst 4 speed shifter. I acquired the car through Matt from work, and in trade I gave him my 1986 Ford Mustang LX.

A terrible design by the way. Back then there was not the option to assume another's loan. The Mustang was financed through Ford Motor Credit. Matt paid on it awhile, but then could not anymore. He tried to hide the car once it was in default, but Lori called Ford and told them where it was since she was still mad at me for turning down her sexual advances all those months back.

I would drive the Firebird across the country back to Illinois. "Were you going to leave without me?" She had asked. "Come along if you want, how did your boyfriend take it?'

"He's not my boyfriend." "I caught you getting ready to screw him! what the hell else am I suppose to call him, and why didn't you just hop on the plane with him?" "Are you planning on leaving in the morning"? She wondered. "Yes, around six." "I will be ready." She wanted to be sure I knew she was going. The rent was without a term contract, so we just walked away.

As much as I admired the car I was now driving, I never had the money to maintain it as need be. A very foolish mistake I would later learn. Pleasant weather in California in the month of March is not the case in places like Colorado. We had barely enough gas money to get us back home to Illinois. Being burnt out on driving and the lack of conversation we were having along the way was putting me to sleep. I spotted a terrible looking dive along the side of the highway literally in the middle of nowhere, for twenty bucks to spend the night. It was cold there with the ice forming on the pavement out front of this glorious establishment; I just wanted to get some rest. We checked in and began to get ready for bed. The phone rings, I answer, but no one is there. A few minutes later there was pounding on the door. "What the hell is going on?!" This was long before I was tuned in to the Other Side, so naturally my mind was thinking we were being followed maybe by one of Robin's suitors, or just some random stalker. I looked out the peep hole and saw no one; though those damn things can't possibly show you every angle. With my 4- inch pocket knife I prepared myself to stab someone if need be. Placing my sweaty hand on the doorknob, I opened it up incredibly fast as if it were a gun draw with my knife ready if they tried rushing me. Absolutely no one was there. Only the hum of the highway traffic going by was to be heard and seen.

It was cold as hell the next morning and no food to be offered at this joint. As we began walking out towards the car, I noticed a stream of liquid under the car that looked fresh. I laid down and slid under the car. I barley fit since it was lowered. I touched the liquid and put it to my nose smelling gas. "Damn it, the fuel line is cracked!" This was all we needed with no money to get it fixed not to mention we were in the middle of a very rural part of the state. I went back inside to inquire about where I might find a mechanic in those parts. The man behind the desk was missing a few teeth, but told me of a guy on some dirt road about a mile down the way. "Yeah, just turn out here to you're right, then make a quick left and drive on down till you see the old sign post with the reflectors all over it and there you will see a little aluminum garage." *Could I be any further from civilization at this moment?* I thought. I thanked him for the tip, and we were on our way. Just like the missing tooth man said, his directions were precise. With fuel still leaking out of my gas line on to the ground we pulled up in the rumbling car that resembled a race car without a number on the side. A taller heavy- set man with slicked back grey hair and wearing black and white striped overalls came walking out of the garage wiping his hands with a shop rag. "Howdy folks." Were his words. "Hello." We both managed to say together. "You got a pretty low car there, fella." "Yes, sir it is." I was glad to hear him call me fella. "What seems to be the problem?" He asked. "The fuel line is leaking; can you fix it?" "Let me take a look at it and we'll go from there." He asked me to pull in up closer so he could put it up on the lift knowing there was no way he was going to get himself even close to getting under the car. We waited and watched him fooling with the line, and about fifteen minutes later he said "She's done." "That's great! um, how much do I owe you?" "Five bucks." Was his response. I couldn't believe it; did he know I didn't have a dime extra? Could he have been an angel in overalls? I thanked him and have never forgotten that man even after all these years.

As we continued on our way toward Illinois, I knew that nothing was going to be any different with my parents even though I had changed my name legally, that certainly was not enough for them to see me as anything other than what I appeared to those who knew me, a masculine female. I still had Robin believing I was some kind of physically twisted guy, and that's what I held on to for my sanity. Even though Robin and I played the couple game in California and on the road, I told her it was not a possibility with my parents. Therefore, I would be dropping her off at her mom's house in Marseilles before I went back to where my parents now lived in the house where I had my first major paranormal experience.

I hadn't been gone long enough yet from Ottawa for it to still not feel like home, but I felt like an outsider for sure. Driving up to this house that I would now find my mother in felt strange; since it was not where I grew up. My mom had told me back when they moved into this house that she had cried when she and my dad were pulling away from the house on Hillside Ave with their final trip of 21 years of belongings. I was greeted with a slight hug upon the door opening by my mother. I could read the displeasing look on her face as to the way I still looked like a gender wreck. We went and sat in the downstairs kitchen, and I again tried to describe to her how it was that I felt and that I simply could not continue to live the rest of my life as a woman I felt I was not. "But you were born a girl." she said. "Mistakes can happen mom before birth." "God does not make mistakes." "I didn't say He did, and I don't believe He does either; it's just not that simple of a situation, and realize now that I am one of many mom." "Do you have any idea what you have put me through? the questions I am now asked about you being a boy while I am at the grocery store?" "I am sorry mom, I won't be here too long, and then I will be headed back to California, San Diego maybe." "I'm going to go see dad at the station". With that I left to drive just a few minutes now to the gas station, Santucci Shell that was now a Mobil. I never did know the reason of the fallout my dad had with Shell that had made him to switch to Mobil.

As I pulled up in a kind of car that was rarely seen, my dad motioned me to drive it in to the bay so he could take a look at it. "Hey beebs." *he is still calling me that even now.* "Where did you get this? Do you know how rare this car is?" "I switched cars with a friend of mine, and no I did not know of its rarity." I replied. "Well keep it as long as you can because this one here, they made less than 1,000 models." "I plan on it, dad, thanks for the tip." I was home for no more than a week, I simply could not handle being around my parents at that point, with my mom constantly making me feel incredibly inadequate, and my dad just being in denial over the fact I am a guy on the inside. He went as far as trying to set me up with a younger friend of his. *What was he thinking?* My dad loved me I know, he accepted me pretty much for who I was, unlike my mom. He just didn't understand. Neither of them did.

The night before Robin and me were set to leave, I was downstairs watching TV when my dad had come home from work. He came down the stairs and stopped midway. "I don't feel too good beebs." That would be the last time I would see him, ever.

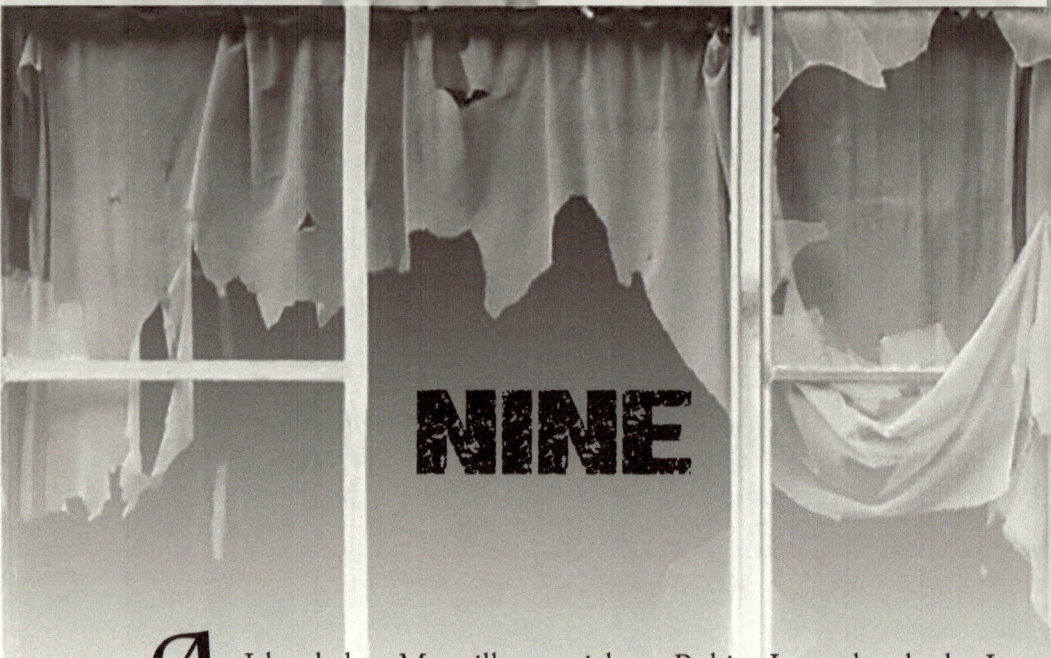

NINE

*A*s I headed to Marseilles to pick up Robin, I wondered why I even was. Why don't I just go without her? Our relationship was not a good one by any means but there was something each of us gained by being together. Since Robin's family did not know me, though her mom knew who my family was, I was able to go by and get her without the whole awkwardness of them looking at me wondering what I was. Her mother was very nice to me, and her sister apparently was not afraid to say how good looking I was and had instantly formed a crush on me based solely on one look. It's all good for an ego I thought as we bid our goodbyes and were off to San Diego.

As we were approaching St Louis, Missouri I, for no reason known to man blurted out "Let's stay in St Louis." Equally as strange, Robin did not object. Again, what was I thinking? We drove in to the downtown area and found a place to stay for the night after we got a bite to eat. The following day first thing in the morning, I set out to get a newspaper to find a place to live. I found an ad with an attractive price for the monthly rent, so I called. "Hello?" said the elderly sounding woman on the line. "Yes, hello; I was calling about the add for the apartment, is it still available?" "Why yes, are you interested in seeing it?" "Can you meet us there today? we are in a motel." With that she gave me the address and agreed to meet us in an hour.

Back then we had to use city maps to find a street. We had arrived before the kind sounding woman which gave us time to assess the area.

It was a two- story old house split into two apartments. The top floor was already rented by someone who owned a 1977 Camaro with white house paint on it. Who does such a thing? The house was made of brick and at least eighty years old at the time. She pulled up and noticed us sitting on the steps. As she walked towards us, she asked; "Have you two been waiting long?" "Just a few minutes." I told her. She walked up the steps past us and opened the big wooden door that was entirely filled with glass, like a store front. It opened to a foyer with hard wood floors and two metal mail boxes side by side for each unit. There was a wooden staircase curving to the left at the top leading to the upstairs apartment where "House Paint" lived, and a door to the immediate left was to the apartment that we were going to look at. Upon entering, the front room had a window to the street, a steam heat iron pipe system, a fireplace, and a little scooped out alcove in the corner on the opposite wall where a phone must have sat some time ago. The archway led to what would have been the dining room back when it was a grander home, but would serve as a bedroom, with the coat closet becoming the only closet. Off that room was the kitchen to the left and a tiny bathroom to the right. We told her we would take it, since it was fine and we really didn't feel like looking all day for another place, ending up in another motel for another night. Again, based on trust, I assured the woman we would have jobs within a week's time.

We had very little to move in, just clothes and a few knick-knacks. Again, we had to rent furniture and find a bed. After we settled in it was off to find a job with Pizza Hut again making the most sense as to where to start. We found one not too far from where we were now living, so we went in and found they were hiring. We both sat down and filled out applications. There was a tall skinny black guy who seemed to be running the place but was not the manager. More like a shift supervisor. He seemed to be taken with the both of us when we sat down with him in a booth. He was very friendly, even a bit funny. Upon review of both our applications we were hired on the spot since they were in need for both a cook and waitress. "Can you both start tomorrow?" He asked. We both responded in unison "Yes." We were both given the same highly attractive brown polyester pants and aprons and went through the paper application process so that it could be sent off to their corporate office.

I would be working mornings and be trained by the tall one who just hired us. I would be proofing the dough for the pan pizzas along with the rest of the behind-the-scenes pizza prep that goes on in kitchens from coast to coast. The tall man's name was Steve, he must have grown up in St Louis. He was possibly eight or so years older than me, and very athletic; at least when it came to running. He lived in an old house across the street from Pizza Hut. The street consisted of four lanes of traffic with two lanes on either side of the median. One day he says to me, "I can run across the street and into my house before the door to this place closes." "Prove it." He put down the stack of medium sized pizza pans he was holding and walked over to the front door, with me following him. He instructed me to open the door all the way up and just let go of it the same time he took off. He prepared himself, putting himself in a sprinters' stance, and the very moment my hand left the door he was off like a shot, as if he was on a racetrack and had heard the sound of the gun. I watched the man fly almost as if his feet barely touched the ground as he moved somehow through the traffic lanes without killing himself. The house was set up on a hill with three very high cement steps to the porch. As he grabbed his own screen door, the door to Pizza Hut came to a close. *Holy shit, he did it.* I was impressed, and I don't say that very often. We became co-working friends, though I never knew much about his life other than he had a few kids and lived in his mom's house. Once I became comfortable with him, I told him my completely made-up strange story about needing a sperm donor to counteract my "evil juices" since I wasn't about to reveal my true biological identity.

For whatever reason we decided to try again to become parents. What were we thinking? What was I thinking? I wanted so badly to play the part of not only a man, but a father as well, or so I thought. I discussed with Robin that I had told Steve of my strange dilemma. I doubt they really believed me, but it was some strange mental shield for me. He was totally fine with what it was I was asking him to do. Come to our place, jack off into a plastic cup, and we will take it from there. I don't recall paying him, but it's possible. We tried this type of fertilization a few times with no luck, just as before with the guy back in Riverside. She never became pregnant. Maybe that was a sign then? That it wasn't meant to be, or shouldn't? Finally, out of frustration we basically asked Steve to just have plain old sex with her. He did not hesitate at the offer. This was arranged around her ovulation cycle naturally, and after a couple of times, she did indeed become pregnant.

At the time, I never gave a lot of thought about the child being mixed, and me being Italian. Logically I'm sure Robin knew I could not actually be the biological father, though the child *would* be mine was mind blowing enough. Four months into the pregnancy it was discovered that Robin was Rh negative and the donor was Rh positive.

This combination results in what is known as the Rh factor. The mother's and baby's blood types are not compatible. This can cause the mother's body to reject the fetus. Luckily there was a simple injection given to Robin so there were no negative side effects.

During Robin's pregnancy, Steve never tried to interfere with what was a charade.

Not to my knowledge anyway. The months past until it was time with all the baby essentials now at hand, we were ready. Early one morning I was awakened by an unusual sound of rustling coming from the tiny closet in our room. I opened my eyes to see Robin vigorously sorting and moving things inside of the small space, while she gathered some personal items and put them into an overnight bag. "What are you doing?" I inquired.

"It's time to go now, the baby is coming, the contractions are getting closer and closer!" I almost fell out of bed as I hurried along to get dressed and throw the newly purchased car seat in the backseat of the car.

I called Susan, our new friend from Rocky Rococo's Pizza where I now worked over in St Charles. I interviewed there a few months prior to the baby's birth since it paid more, and Robin was going to be off work awhile. It was a new building at the time and they had to staff it. I was hired on the spot as a shift supervisor, more in the kitchen than the front of the store and got along pretty well with everyone who worked there. One particular day the assistant manager on duty called me into the extremely tiny office which consisted of a built in 4x6 desk and a black rolling chair, though there was nowhere to roll. A four-drawer filing cabinet was on the opposite side from the desk which then left maybe four feet between the cabinet and the wall opposite of that. She said she needed to show me something as I followed her into the cramped space. She shut the door behind me, shoved me up against the only wall space there was and planted her lips on mine kissing me as hard as she could hoping I would respond in the same way. I was more shocked than anything, and certainly didn't see it coming.

I usually have a pretty good sense when someone is attracted to me, but I missed this one. After pushing her away from me I asked; "What the hell are you doing?!" "I thought you would be open to it, you're not into Robin, that is what you said, and now I feel like an idiot!" "I'm not in love with her, that is true; don't feel stupid, you just caught me off guard." "Then you are interested in us having something?" "No, not really, but I'm flattered if that helps any." "Please don't tell Shane or Mick, I will be fired." "I won't." I assured her. Mick hired me; he ran the whole store while Shane was the assistant. He had a girlfriend that also worked there that unfortunately I was attracted to, Elena. I remember she was nineteen, so that would have made me twenty-three. What I felt for her, I never felt for Robin. Love is blind that's for sure.

TEN

"Hello?" said the familiar woman's voice. "Susan, its time, can you meet us at the hospital?" "Yes, of Course!" Susan had taken Robin and me under a kind of parental wing. She had a couple of kids, her son was five years younger than me, so I was still in the age range she could have been my mother. We pretended she was during the hospital part of all of this. When a baby is about to be born it feels as though time freezes in that moment. Upon check in, Robin was wheeled to a private birthing room. Some hospitals offer this luxury instead of the cold metal table that sits under the incredibly blinding bright lights where to witness such a feat. I watched while several nurses busy themselves arranging metal implements and rolling in emergency equipment if needed. It was clear Robin was in a lot of pain at this point, the doctor had now made her way to the room. "Good morning, are you ready to have a baby?" I wasn't sure how to answer that so I kept silent while Robin continued to wince in pain. Susan was there on the other side of the bed dressed like me in the yellow gown attire for this fair morning. Time was running out for any form of pain block since the doctor said Robin was dilated already to five centimeters. "Robin, breathe and start pushing." said the very calm doctor. At this point I went into some kind of trance, not prepared for what was next and feeling as though time did actually stop.

After she pushed hard enough to break several blood vessels, this tiny olive colored being emerged from Robin's body, silent but healthy. She was beautiful, with an eye color I had never seen in my life. Violet was what they looked like. The doctor cut the cord; that was not something I was interested in doing. Upon inspection this child could have very well been my own biological one at a glance. Light olive colored skin, like I am with dark hair. I was listed on the birth certificate as her father, and it would remain that way for years. It was October, 1988, with Christmas right around the corner. With all the baby hoopla behind us, the birth part anyway, I was back to work. Happy that Robin seemed happy with a baby now, which is what she wanted. I wanted Elena.

Mistletoe hung in the doorway to the kitchen at work, and every chance I had I would stop Elena in the doorway as she began to pass through and ask her to stand under it so I could kiss her. She would just laugh, and carry on. This went on for the entire month of November, the continuous flirting back and forth, even when Shane was there. He lived in a house with a few other guys splitting the rent, I'm sure. They were having a party one night after work, so Elena asked me if I wanted to go and if I might pick her up. I agreed naturally. She gave me her address along with directions and I told her I would be there right after we closed to pick her up. "There will be a couple of my friends with me, can they ride over too?" "Sure." I said, anything to get her in my car I thought. When I pulled up to her house, she was waiting outside with two friends just as she had mentioned would be coming along. She had a car, a Pontiac Fierro, but those only seat two and couldn't accommodate her second friend was the reason I was asked to pick them all up. All three of them climbed in the backseat, with Elena sitting behind me. As she navigated me to our destination, she became physical with me from the backseat.

She put her arms around my shoulders and chest, which both turned me on, and made me panic at the same time. Thank God she never started feeling down further to discover the ace bandage that was binding what I was hiding from the world. That would have been tragic. I was surprised by what she was doing, letting me know she was interested.

We arrived at the house where the party had been in full swing for quite some time. There must have been close to twenty people there. Shane seemed to be slightly tipsy along with most everyone else. I didn't drink, so I skipped the offers of booze. The girls stayed near the kitchen popping open beers and wine coolers while I took it upon myself to take a self guided tour of the house. There was a loft area I found interesting with a bed and low lighting. Posters all over the walls that I couldn't quite make out what any of them were. While I was laying on the bed, I was wondering whose area it was. I just listened to the din of the crowd downstairs, along with the droning sound of the music.

Eventually Elena had made her way up to this room finding me on the bed and plopped down next to me. *My God how much I wanted her.* It would never be, my secret was in the way. She would never understand, no one would understand. She had clearly been drinking, but not drunk, just a little looser than usual. She definitely had to have been keeping tabs on Shane in order to spend such time with me in that moment. She laid down on her side beside me. I was on my back, incredibly nervous having to stay alert to where she might put her hands. I wanted her so very much to touch me, but then not. The bulge in my pants was not what she would expect if she were to unzip my pants. If things became physical, I would have to take complete control of her hands. She really wasn't that forward of a girl, just a little flirty for now. As I kept my chest guarded, she put her hand on the lower part of my stomach; right above what I'm sure she thought was an impending erection. If she were to put her hand on it, it would be fine as long as she didn't go unbuttoning or unzipping. In my mind I was thinking if she wanted to screw me then I would just have to do the same as always and insist that my clothes stay on, while she would have to strip off her jeans and underwear. The heat from my body kept the erection in my pants realistic enough to get by with. Just as she was beginning to move her hand down toward what was hard and ready for action, my own bigger than normal "part" was now throbbing with its own tiny attached erection. Then someone from down the stairs called her name, saying that Shane was looking for her. I bet he was. "Just wait here Marco, I will be back." "As much as I would like to stay, I'm going to go; I will see you at work." On my drive home I thought, what was she thinking? Was she going to attempt to actually have sex with me with her boyfriend and a whole house of people just down the stairs? I forced my mind from continuing to push the replay button of what just happened as I headed home to Robin and the baby, wondering what I was going to do about my messed-up identity crisis. This reminded me I needed to contact the woman in Palo Alto especially now that I was living in Missouri at this time. I was accepted into the program and had to get out there to be evaluated in person before anything else could move forward.

The next morning, I called the clinic explaining how I was now living in Missouri but would still like to make the trip to be seen. They booked my appointment for the end of May in 1989, which gave me time to come up with the money required to be seen there and make the trip back to California. In the meantime, we moved to St Charles into a little trailer in a family type park. We needed a second bedroom for the baby. As small as it was, it was her own room.

It was becoming increasingly harder to work at Rocky Rococo's with Elena. The sexual tension between us grew every day. Two weeks before I was to take the Palo Alto trip, I turned in my resignation.

The night before we were to leave, I asked Elena to meet me at the park since I knew I would never see her again. I arrived before her, so I sat in my car watching the raindrops start to hit the windshield very lightly, then turning into a steady rain. It was almost dark now and I was hoping she didn't change her mind. Just then the little silver Fierro pulled up next to my car. I got out and walked to her car door. "Hey, how are you?" I asked. "I'm good; and you?" "Alright I guess." I had told her as we began to walk towards the trees where there was a bunch of cut logs stacked up. I took her hands in mine and just looked at her face to face as the rain began coming down harder now. There really were no words at this point, only wonder of what might have, or could have been. I then took her face into my hands and kissed her for a good long while. It was the first time, and it would be the last. I watched her walk away, and waited until she drove away before I went home myself. When I walked in the door Robin asked me where I had been. "Just out, we are leaving early in the morning, so I'm going to get ready for bed."

Six a.m. came quickly, we only packed a couple of bags the night before knowing this was going to be a turnaround trip even with the far distance that needed to be driven. At the time Palo Alto was one of very few places to seek help with gender issues so I really didn't feel I had much of a choice. The baby was five months old now and wasn't one to dislike riding in a car, thank God, though I don't recall what the reason may have been that I just didn't take the trip alone since we were going to be back in less than a week. We made it all the way to just inside the border of Wyoming that first night, and then into Nevada the second night. I was pretty wiped out at this point, but just knowing I would be in the office the next day made it all worth it.

At the crack of dawn, the following day I got up to get ready for my life to change that very day, while Robin and the baby slept. I went into the bathroom, bound my chest as tight as I could, admired the bulge in my pants, and applied the five o'clock shadow to my top lip appearing to be just the slightest stubble growth with the magic pencil I had taken from my mom's make up two years ago.

When I came from the bathroom Robin was changing the baby and then began to gather our things together for this impending destination that had become far overdue for me. Even though she didn't understand it, she knew how incredibly important it was I show up there. My appointment was set for the late afternoon given the distance I was driving so as to not worry about being late. After all it was still almost another five hundred miles or so, and a drive through Yosemite National Park before arriving. This would mean the only stops would be for gas and bathroom facilities. All eating would have to be done in the car while moving. The anticipation was killing me by this time, the prospect of being in a place where there were people who actually understood someone like me.

When we arrived, we were greeted by a blonde-haired woman. "Marco?" "Yes." "How long have you been on Testosterone?" "I'm not." She was quite surprised by that, which made me feel pretty damn good. "Is this your wife?" "Yes, this is Robin." "It's nice to meet you both. Marco, you come with me so we can get started." I followed her back to a private office, where we mostly talked. "Marco, you look very male now even before Testosterone injections, and any kind of surgery, you will have no problem I'm sure making a full transition when you're at that point." She gave me a rundown of how I have to continue to live as a male for a year and a half once starting the hormone therapy, and gave me as much information as she could on doctors across the

United States that preformed SRS (Sex Reassignment Surgery). She contacted the only doctor in St Louis to set me up with testosterone injections making my first appointment the day after we would return to Missouri. As I left her office I felt as if things would be as I wished at some point down the road, the only question was, when?

Heading back home always seems to go quicker than the leaving. I suppose it has something to do with when the anticipation of getting to a destination is over, and now time does not seem to be infinite now. Before we had left for Palo Alto, I had answered some want ads for work since I certainly couldn't afford to be off much more than a week. The answering machine had a few responses back to me asking if I would be interested in an interview. One in particular piqued my interest and I set up an interview for the same day as my first appointment to get my initial testosterone injection to set me on my wat to real manhood. It was a painting company out of St Louis, and I knew I needed to do whatever it took to secure that job. I was a bit nervous on my way to the city, not really knowing what to expect. In the doctor's office it was the typical new patient paperwork. I sat a short while in the waiting room until I was called in by a nurse who escorted me to a room. There really wasn't much to it, other than pulling my pants down and waiting for her to stick me in a butt check. "Every two weeks you need to come back for another shot." "Ok, I will make an appointment then" I said to her while I was pulling my pants back up. *Every two weeks for the rest of my life.* I didn't feel any different while I was driving to the address given on the phone message about the painting job. I mean I knew it would take some time to notice any big changes, but just a twinge or something would have been nice, but not expected.

I drove up to a rather large office building and rode the elevator to the seventh floor. The man behind the desk explained the position was that of a second painter to meet up with the lead guy at any given location. A good majority of the work was between two apartment complexes, which meant it certainly would be steady work. It all sounded good to me, then he proceeded to ask me why he should hire me. In my mind I was thinking, *because I need the job.* Instead, I told him I had painted often, just not getting paid for it, and I believed it was good therapy for the soul. That was good enough for him. He wrote out the address where I was to meet a guy named Bob.

The night before, I had to check to see if I still had white painters' pants and a couple of white t-shirts, a little oversized as to not have to worry about them clinging to what others were unaware of. It was a Monday through Friday gig, and I made enough to pay the bills and support my bi-weekly doctor's visits to receive my shot. Seven months into both this job and my shots I was in one of the bathrooms of an apartment we were painting. While I was cutting in around the big square mirror that hung over the sink, I happened to look at myself a little harder than usual. I stopped what I was doing and looked at the presence of acne on my face. *What have I done?* My skin had always been so perfect and blemish free. My back contained the same horrible scars. This is by far the worst side affect of testosterone. Your body is thrown into puberty regardless of your age, and I was twenty- four.

Just a few days later while we were visiting some odd friends we had, a sheriff had walked up the steps of their trailer and knocked on the door. This can't be a good thing I thought, wondering what Jerry might have done to have the law standing at his door.

Then he opened the door, the officer said; "Is Marco Roselli here?" I was perplexed to say the least, as I walked to meet him, my mind reeling. "Yes sir?" "I regret having to inform you, but your father Carmen Santucci has passed, your wife's mother wanted to be sure you received the news." "Thank you for finding me." At this point in time my mother was not really speaking to me with all of my talk of having a sex change; I changed my name legally, and forced a family upon myself. It was clear that my mom had no intention of informing me of my fathers death, I'm sure to spare her the embarrassment of having to deal with my horrendous existence.

It seems that Robin's mom knew somehow that I may not get the important news, she would have read it for herself in the paper, it was on the front page. The mystery is how they were able to find me at someone else's residence. She would have called the sheriff's department in St Charles since that was where our last address was: the trailer. Again, the question that is unclear to me to this day is how they knew where I was, long before GPS. It eludes me. This meant a trip now to Illinois; I certainly was not going to be excluded no matter what I looked like, and however my mom felt about me. He was my dad no matter what. We left our friends place and went home immediately to pack. This time not only a few bags, but everything we could cram into one of those U-Haul steel boxes that can be strapped to the roof of a car. Although we did not have a clear plan, it was definitely not to return to Missouri.

Within the last twelve months Robin had the outside influence from Darla trying to convince her to leave me, and honestly, I don't know why she never did. We created this life that seems it was never meant to be, and I mean that in every sense of the thought. At the moment I could think of nothing else but getting back home.

ELEVEN

I wasn't sure what to expect when we arrived back to Ottawa. I still couldn't believe my mom didn't even call me to let me know dad had died. We drove right to St Mary's in Naplate, to my dad's funeral which was already in progress. I found the streets lined with over a hundred cars and a packed church. Robin just stayed in the car with the baby while I went in and waited at the back of the church foyer. When the service was over and the fire station began to sound its air horn in honor of my father, the people began to pour out of the church with my mother leading the way. "Mom", I had said as I tried to grab her arm. She just looked at me with complete disdain and disappointment as she continued out the door to the limo hearse that would carry my father's body to the cemetery. I watched as my two brothers and two of my cousins along with two uncles carry the casket out the door.

My cousin Joann came up to me and looked at me for a moment before she said "Cousin?", not really sure if it was me, or maybe just out of shear shock after getting a look at me. I followed the casket out walking to the open car door where my mother sat. Before I could get a word out, she said; "You are not welcome in this car." Apparently, the shame I had caused her was too great. I walked back to my car as the hearse began to roll away, feeling as if I had no existence at all, to anyone there. There were so many cars in the procession, I ended up being very close to the end of the line before I could jump in. No little flag or sticker on my car indicating I was with this huge group. It would be almost a five-mile drive with the longest line of cars this town had ever seen for a funeral that I am aware of. My dad had a lot of friends; no doubt, it looked like a freight train moving through town.

His body would go into the wall inside the mausoleum next to his father Carlo and his mother Mabel. The cemetery sits up on a hillside with perfectly manicured grounds as you wind around the man-made pond dug many years ago deemed "duck pond" for the fact that every year like clockwork ducks migrate there for their season of time. The mausoleum is at the very top of where all roads meet within the cemetery. On this day there were two fire trucks parked opposite of each other with their ladders extended crossing one another like swords in the air paying homage to my father. The cars passed under the site as they drove towards the building at the end of the road. All four sides of the roads were lined with cars making it hard for me to find a spot, ending up parking at the very bottom of the hill. As I walked up towards the building with its grey colored chiseled stone and stained-glass windows, I tried to put the fact behind me that I am going to walk into this building presenting as a man but thought of as a woman. My stomach began to feel sick, now as I was approaching the doors with people jammed in wall to wall. I went unnoticed winding through the crowd while I walked the corridor walls lined with headstones within, until I reached the room where my father's casket was on display closed waiting for the priest to come and say his words. I never did get to see him lying in the casket, since I was purposely made to miss the wake, and most of the funeral.

I stood near my mom though I felt she would rather I did not. She couldn't love me this way, so it seemed. After all the said words of hope and Heaven, and people began to clear out of the tiny room, I approached the casket and took one of the cut roses that had been placed on top. I felt like that was all I had. I didn't even cry, all I felt was detachment. I realized I had accomplished that on my own with leaving home and attempting to live as a man, so there I stood feeling as much of an outsider as could be possible. No one really knew what to say to me as they looked at me, my aunt Anna hugged me slightly, and my cousin's Jaymie and Laura, the sister's of Joann at least said hello. My mom shunned me, totally ashamed, not claiming me as her own.

I am unable to express the kind of grief I felt that day over my mom's behavior as I walked through the walls of people, though feeling good that so many people loved, or at least greatly liked my dad. He was a good guy, just a highly functioning alcoholic.

When I reached the car, I felt there was nothing more to do then get back on the road and begin to head west again. Along the way I told Robin maybe we should just go back to California and skip St Louis. She never seemed to care anymore than I did where we were, so the destination became downtown Riverside to the house of Darla and Walt. They would take us in for a short period of time while I went looking for a job.

I had made a call to Palo Alto telling them I was going back to California and needed a referral to a doctor's office to receive my bi-weekly shot. It would end up being in Costa Mesa. When we arrived, the weather was pleasant as usual for California, Darla was waiting outside for us while we drove down the back alley to park our car.

It was an old two-story Victorian house that served as two residences. They lived on the bottom half of the house. Darla showed us to the room we would stay in so we could put our bags down. I went right out the front door and picked up their newspaper, that still laid in front of the steps leading up to the porch. I scanned the want ads looking for pretty much anything. I came across an ad for a manager in a new pizza place out in Perris. The starting pay was three hundred dollars a week, which was a lot to me. I called and set up an interview for the next day, finding out their office building was right there in the downtown area.

I knew Darla was inside the house telling Robin she needed to get away from me, being that they were still trying to find out my actual origin. I can only imagine the conversations that were coaxed out of Robin by Darla, to get more information to use against me to get her to stay away from me. That night after dinner, Walt started messing around with me, teasing and trying to wrestle by grabbing me around my chest and I began to panic, with the thought he might feel something that didn't seem quite right on a man's body which would then prompt some major questions. I began to sweat as I tried to break free from his grip. Finally, he let go, and I tried to read his face for his thoughts but got nothing.

After that I went to take a shower and get ready for the next morning. I had hoped it would be a productive day pounding the pavement for work. When I came out from the shower, Robin was sitting up on the bed we would share, the baby was asleep. I asked her if she wanted to watch a movie, and she agreed. Halfway through it she began to start touching me in the allowed places, only being my stomach, and the most upper half of my chest. These were the rules. I knew she wanted to have sex with me, it had been a while for sure. Right at that moment Darla knocked and opened the door with a look of shock on her face since we were lying so closely together. What a prude I thought.

Apparently, her talk to Robin earlier hadn't swayed her from her wanting to have sex. As soon as the lights went out under the crack of our door, we tore our clothes off in the darkness. She knew not to even consider touching me; that I was to do all the work. All she had to do was lay there and enjoy it, and that she did. Through her pleasure, came mine as well.

In the morning I headed over to the office building for my interview and met with two Middle Eastern men who were cousins. They owned the business together and were conducting the management interviews that day to staff the store they had franchised. I ended up convincing them both I was capable of running a tiny little takeout pizza place. It was built in a field right off the freeway; nothing else was around it. It was probably cheap land at the time. They hired me on the spot, and then we took a ride to the store. It was brand new, due to open in two weeks. At the same time, we also were moving to an apartment to get away from Darla.

I was to do the in-person interviewing of the people that were set up over the phone through the office. Most of the people I hired were young, though there was one older woman I hired for the front, I knew she would do well with customers at the counter.

She was a very sweet lady. Things went fine for awhile, outside of a few verbal fights I ended up in with one of the owners. I hate when people get in my face. If that hadn't been enough of a reason to start looking for a different job fairly soon, an even bigger one was yet to come.

The only car we had at the time was in need of a smog check, so Robin dropped me off at work and would come back that night with the baby right before closing to pick me up.

This building only had a front door, with the counter right in front of that, the kitchen was off to the left along with a small office and large walk-in cooler which was where the arguments took place between me and the Middle Eastern guy. After Robin and the baby had arrived to pick me up, I was finishing the deposit in the office when Miguel called for me across the small building, "Hey boss, can you unlock the door for me to take the trash out?" "I'll be right there, just a minute." After dropping the deposit into the safe, I walked to the front passing my few closing employees who were cleaning up after a busy night, I found Miguel patiently waiting for me at the door with a giant trash bag slung over his shoulder. As I turned the key in the lock to open the door, I pushed it allowing Miguel just enough clearance to get around me. When he turned to the right into the darkness, he stopped short, and started backing up back towards the door along with a skinny tall black guy forcing both of us back into the store while shoving a pistol up against my head telling me I needed to give him all the money in the safe. He seemed to know of its exact location.

When he spotted the baby, he turned the gun on her assuming this would make it even a higher threat, while making everyone in the store line up several feet back behind me and the safe. I went right to dialing in the combination to open the safe, but with all of his yammering and threats, I watched myself spin right past the second number while he now had the gun on my back, waving his other hand around frantically ready to blow me away if I didn't give him what he wanted. When I realized my egregious error, I knew I was going to have to clear out the dial and start all over again with the combination. When I got to the first number again, he said, "COME ON MAN! WHAT'S TAKING SO LONG!!" All of a sudden, I heard a click, it just opened, without the entire combination. I handed him the deposit bag I had put in there not long before this moment which contained 1,400.00 cash. He looked at me and said; "Where's the rest?!" "That's all there is." I told him. He looked at all of us while waving the gun around as he backed out of the store. I watched him run through the open field into the darkness of the night while I locked the door. Outside of being a bit shaken from it all, everyone was fine. I called the police and the owners now with everyone on their way. Afterwards we realized there was a 400.00 bank hidden in a compartment he didn't get, that I had just forgotten about. To this day I know that safe was opened by God himself. There is simply no other possibility. Safes don't open on their own midway into dialing a combination. I gave these guys a week's notice, and made plans yet again to go back to Illinois, though I had no idea why, and was not prepared for what was to come.

TWELVE

Driving miles upon miles back home I contemplated…What is home? Where you were born? Where you grew up? A place where you may or may not die? Does it matter anymore? As I pondered these thoughts an hour and a half west of Illinois, what was about to happen to me would change my life in ways I never signed up for. Robin and I never really talked much anymore, it almost seemed like one of us was waiting for the other to just walk away without a word. We both certainly had plenty of opportunities to do so over the last three years. Staring out at the never-ending stretch of road before me, I heard in my left ear a male voice clear as a bell ask, "Do you know who you are?" I instinctively looked at the radio knowing it was not on. I then asked Robin, "Did you hear that?" "Hear what?" She said while she tore herself away from her own continuous stare out the window from her side of the car. "That voice…like he was right here in this car." "I never heard a thing." She insisted.

In that split second of that very moment, I knew it had to stop. This voice made me do a complete 180 at the drop of a hat. With my religious upbringing, I assumed it could only have been the voice of God. Even though as a child I did hear disembodied voices every now and again, but this was different. I associated this voice as the Supreme Being of the universe. Who else would ask me such a question? The most perplexing part of it all, was that my mind was altered in that moment to dump my male identity and come to terms with who and what I was born. I was thinking somewhere in the back of my mind that idea to be preposterous, and the more I tried to fight the thought out of my head, the stronger it became, as if I had no control. Yeah, only God can do that, not some random spirit, trust me on that.

I turned to Robin and told her what I had to do but didn't elaborate on what had just happened to me. "I have to drop you and the baby off at your mom's for good. We can't be together, it's not right. I have to go home and apologize to my mom for what I've put her through, and deal with the gender in which I was born." She never said a word as we drove on towards home, I guess because she finally got the answer she had started to suspect, and I had been unwilling to share my guarded secret. It was like a switch I never flipped. I still didn't understand but could only do what I felt compelled to do at that moment. When pulling into Robin's mother's driveway I just wanted to get them out of my car as quick as I could, and maybe I could forget all of it even happened. I actually sped away from there like it was the scene of a crime and set my sights on getting back to my mom's house seven miles away.

I pulled up to the house just as my mom finished pulling her car into the garage. I jumped out of my car and ran up the driveway ducking under the garage door before it closed completely. She never saw me until she was getting out of her car as I stood right there before her. "Mom?" "OHH!! you scared me." She was always a bit jumpy anyway. "Mom, I'm back, and I'm sorry for everything I did to upset you, it's over, and I'm going to change my name back." "Thank God! Now what about you being married to Robin?

We will have to get it annulled; I will pay for it." "Thanks mom." As we walked in the house, I heard her immediately get on the phone and call her sister Sharon. "She's finally come to her senses." I heard her say as I walked down the stairs to take a shower, and remove all the extra body hair I had acquired from the testosterone I was on for just under a year and a half.

Even though my voice was already a little deeper than most girls, it did drop an octave or so, which is irreversible. The only reason I felt at ease at all was because I was making my mom happy. I really wasn't too sure how I felt about it myself just yet, and it would take a little time for my body to bounce back and have a normal estrogen level again, if I ever did have one before. The absence of the testosterone would give me back my good skin, that was for sure.

The first week or so I hung out with my mom, trying to become closer to her which was never easy. We took care of the annulment and changing my name back at her lawyers' office in town. I'm sure she felt that was money well spent. I then cancelled the consultation that was scheduled for me in Colorado to prepare for a double mastectomy. That had cut all ties with me receiving any medical treatment pertaining to becoming a man. It was awkward for me now being home, not feeling like there was anyone to hang out with at this point. I ran into Paul that lived next door to us when I was growing up. He was about eight years older than me. He asked me if I wanted to go to this club with him and a friend. This seemed very strange since we didn't really talk when we were younger; it must have been the age difference back then. Clubs were not my scene, but I went just to have something to do. I had never been to this small, converted warehouse, thinking it must have been a new business since I hadn't been gone that long. It was the typical bar with loud music playing. There was low lighting and some flashing lights for entertainment purposes to go with the dance floor area. This guy walks up to me and says, "Remember me?" "Luke, right?" I answered. "Yea, from Home Economics class." "Yes, I remember you; that does seem awhile ago now." I really remembered him as being kind of awkward, and not too popular of a guy. He was not super attractive, and he didn't play any sports. He was very nice, and since I had to throw myself into the typical female role, I thought, "why not with him?". This was yet another strange thought I cannot explain. In the back of my mind, biologically thinking, if I were to have a baby, this would be the only way for me to stay on the female track, without jumping back on the male track. Insane idea, but that was all I could come up with. Like I said, a switch was flipped; I was having thoughts I had never entertained prior.

We "dated" if I must call it that; he was the first guy I had sex with. Shit…writing these words are extremely difficult, and I'm just getting started. Due to the fact that my body was now coming down off the testosterone, it unfortunately took a total of three incredibly uncomfortable times having sex with him in order to conceive. After that I was seriously done with being around him, he drove me nuts with his odd self, along with his excessive habits. He actually asked me to marry him because of the situation. I told him he was crazy, while I pointed out all the reasons that it was a very bad idea. First of all, he drank and smoked: two things I have never tolerated well all the way back to my childhood. Both my parents smoked, and the memories of sitting in the back seat of our maroon Oldsmobile 98, with all the windows rolled up filling my lungs with the smoke will never leave me.

When I announced this news to my mom it was over dinner. "Mom, I'm going to have a baby." Her mouth fell open while the spaghetti slid off her fork. She was in complete shock, and I have to agree it was just that…shocking. Going from living as a man, to announcing I was going to have a child was a bit much for her. Naturally, she suggested we get married, after all that was the right thing to do. For who? I thought. Those who need someone to take care of them? I needed no one to do any such thing. I was on a quest to be what it seemed I was born; female. I still wondered where this was all coming from. I was very impulsive, I still am, but this was so far out of what I ever thought I was capable of.

As the weeks passed, the weather changed as did my body. I was working and making decent enough money, I had an upstairs apartment I lived in now, and Luke would come over and annoy me. My mind was starting to tip back toward who I really was and needed to be. This was clear when I had fallen down on a patch of ice when getting into my car and said, "Oh well." Thinking if something happens to the baby, no big deal.

Subconsciously I didn't want it to happen, but giving birth was something I had never planned or desired to do. I was forcing myself into a situation and could not turn back from. Going through the motions of being a woman I so despised, and mentally was never able to accept, was going to be a very hard road to travel.

I attempted to form more of a relationship with my mother. I decided, yet again, to go back to California. Only this time my mom rode out there with me and would fly back after a couple of days. Oddly enough Robin and I had remained friends and she too had gone back to

California on her own with her daughter who was now two. She had an apartment in Perris and agreed I could stay with her awhile. It was April 1991, three months until this baby would be born. It took me and my mom six whole days to drive from Illinois to California. Back then she still had the strength to shop so we ended up stopping a lot along the way in the major cities to do just that.

There was also the excitement of wildfires jumping across the interstate at one point stopping traffic as the flames danced across both sides of the roads going in opposite directions of each other keeping things interesting; the wind is a mighty thing. When we arrived at Robin's apartment, I dropped off my things, then we all went together to find a place to get something to eat. Along the way my mother became incredibly irritated at how late it was for going to dinner. She began to argue with me that dinner, which she called "supper", is never served so late in Illinois. I told her that in California it is very common for people to eat after six o'clock. We began to argue in front of Robin. I could not believe her insensitivity to others in the car and just her sheer rudeness. She ended up walking out of the restaurant we had chosen and taking a cab to the hotel she had booked from home. She left the next day on a flight back to Chicago. Unexplainable behavior.

Robin and I spent the next couple of weeks getting reacquainted, trying not to make it seem awkward. I went back to the same church in Riverside as I had been to when presenting as a male only a few years ago. No one could have possibly recognized me, I knew that. It was strange though seeing people that knew me as Marco.

I submerged myself into going to church and doing Bible studies, I had to stay on the right path. I refused to watch any talk show or any other kind of show at all pertaining to transgendered people. I couldn't take the chance of allowing that craving to return. I was going to be a mother; nothing could change that reality now. Throughout the pregnancy I felt pretty normal. I never got sick, just tired of waiting. I wasn't working at the time, and with no insurance I was on Medi-Cal, (California state aid.) When I was in Illinois and had gone to the initial appointment in the beginning of all this, the doctor was some old man who was way too rough with that horrific pelvic exam crap one has to go through, so I had always requested women physicians once I got back to California.

July 4th we were at Darla's sisters' house which was very close to Mt Rubidoux, where the yearly fireworks were shot off in Riverside. Her yard offered a perfect view without the crowd. It was a whole day's event with food and volleyball, which I did participate having no problem getting myself up off the ground to spike the ball, as bystanders were amazed. A bit later that night the contractions had started and were pretty strong, making me wonder if this baby might be born on the fourth of July.

Through these last four months Robin and I got along well as friends considering our volatile relationship of our past. Darla had stayed friends with me as well since I had "seen the light" and obeyed God now, as far as she was concerned. Since I was adhering to the gender in which I was born and had stopped wanting to change my body. Even though I was about to give birth without any man around to take care of me, Darla didn't condemn me for that.

Five days later, Robin was at work, I was home with her daughter baking cookies. Yes, really, I was. Not feeling a thing, a gush of water streamed down my legs. That was a big enough sign for me to start making the phone calls. I ended up having to call Darla to come and take me to the hospital which was in Riverside, almost a half an hour away.

My car was totaled from some drunken jack ass that rear ended me just a couple of weeks before. While I waited for Darla, I found myself having to keep a bath towel between my legs with all the fluid I was now losing. When she arrived, we had to gather Robin's daughter and take her with us since her mother would have to meet us there. I put the towel on the cloth seat (not good) trying to save it from the inevitable leaking that would take place during the ride.

Along the way the contractions became closer and closer. Now I was uncomfortable and started to become nervous over this whole thing. "I'm sorry about the seat." I had told her. "Don't worry about that, let's just get you there." I did appreciate her support, again another odd moment for me. In my mind the images that were flying past, the fact that only one year ago I was living as a man, ready to embark on sex reassignment surgery without hesitation. How did this all happen? I had no answer for myself, or anyone else. The people that surrounded me that knew, simply said it was what God wanted me to do. I accepted that and went with it, as far out of my comfort zone as it was.

By the time we reached the hospital I was in enough pain, and the contractions were pretty close so I was in no mood to sit, and that was the game plan in this hospital. It was the community hospital that was well over one hundred years old, with many horrible stories of unnecessary deaths of both adults and unborn children throughout the years.

Poor health care practices along with a large psych ward, I believe, is the reason for the known paranormal events that have taken place on the property, but that is another story.

I did end up having to sit for awhile on one of the hard plastic seats I continued to leak all over. Finally, almost an hour later I was wheeled to an area to disrobe to be placed on a bed within an operating room that fit the Hollywood version of a horror movie with its cold stainless steel and bright lights blinding me. Many nurses gathered around me assessing my physical state. I was asked if I wanted an epidural into the spine, I gladly said yes while the pain intensified. When the doctor reached the room, she explained to me now that I was numb, she would be telling me when to push. That sounded easy enough I thought. Not knowing the first thing about giving birth, it was beginning to become more complicated as my body was wanting to get it over with while the doctor was telling me not to push when I felt the need to. Eight hours from the time my water broke the baby was born.

THIRTEEN

She cried with her first breath as they laid her on me, then she was quiet. They took her for only a few moments to wash and wrap her up, then brought her back to me. She was beautiful, and at that very moment my life changed, even more with the fact of knowing that this tiny person knew only me to depend on for survival. Our bond was instant, a feeling very hard to describe. Even though I had assumed I would have a boy since I figured what the heck would I do with a girl? It didn't matter, she was mine. I only had one girl's name picked out just in case. Her name would be Mariah. Simply because I didn't like many girl names enough to pin it to them for their entire life. Mariah Cary had been discovered, and began to climb the music charts, leading me to see her first video a few months prior and thought if the baby happens to be a girl, that would be her name. I had never heard the name before, and I liked it. Her middle name would represent my mother's Catholic name taken on when one has their First Communion, Mariah Katherine Santucci. I thought it had a nice flow to it.

They came and took her from me again, telling me she would be in the nursery while I rested. There were so many babies born that day, or at least the day before since it was early morning hours when she was born, there was no room to put me in. That's right, I was pushed outside the OR doors into the hallway to sleep. I passed out and slept for several hours. Eventually I woke up to see Robin waiting to help me get out of there.

When we got back to the apartment, Robin was very indifferent towards me. This behavior continued and I never understood it. It was almost like she was jealous, though I don't know about what.

Now that I had a child, I needed to find a way to make money and not leave Mariah with sitters. That was not going to be part of my plan in raising her. Darla suggested looking at the want ads for a live in position in someone's home. At first, I thought that was ridiculous living with people I did not know, but the more I thought about it the more it made perfect sense. Watch someone's kids while they went off to work, get paid and have free rent with my child by my side. I started making calls and setting up interviews. After a couple of offers that I rejected, I called and talked to a woman who had two boys, five and seven. Her voice over the phone was a bit sultry and I learned later she thought mine reminded her of a truck driver, what ever that was supposed to mean. While we talked on the phone, I felt pretty comfortable with this woman, and was actually looking forward to meeting her. She was a recently divorced, now single mom, was a nurse with a schedule that included several odd shifts at any given time. A live-in person was a must for her. She had others already to this point; currently a young woman at the time was leaving, making the need of a replacement rather urgent was the reason for her ad.

The next night I drove to her house that was still in Riverside bordering Norco. Naturally I had Mariah with me, she was three months old and was sick with her first cold, which I believed she got since the room we were sleeping in had no heat and was a bit drafty.

Driving down Arlington Avenue I reached the start of the neighborhoods where people could have some types of livestock. There was actually an ostrich farm at the base of the road that would lead me to this woman's home. Rounding the corner, the homes were nice middle-class ones for the most part; it seemed like a decent area.

I pulled into the driveway and proceeded to gather up Mariah and the diaper bag.

As I walked to the door, I saw a smaller head peeking out behind the curtain in the living room. Before I rang the doorbell the door was opening already by a little blonde boy. "Hi." he said. "Come in, I will get my mom. He must have been the five-year old I thought. I sat on the couch with Mariah on my lap. I was very curious as to what this woman looked like after hearing her speak. The little blond boy returned from the den with his mother. Not what I had expected, at all. "Hello, I'm Susan." "Good to meet you". I had said, almost speechless. It was certainly one of those moments that reminded me how while listening to a radio station, hearing the voice on the air and getting a mental picture of what they look like. More times than not, we are dead wrong on our perception of how the person will look when we see them, whether it's in person or only a photo. Her face was fine; it was just the whole overweight thing that had caught me completely off guard. I was thinking she could rack up some serious money doing phone sex with that voice. We sat and talked a good hour at least, she commented on how well-behaved Mariah was, even in her misery. We really did get along quite well so she offered me the job, and I took it. The little blonde boy came in and out of the room several times, being very curious and telling me that the house was clean since we were coming over.

We moved in that same weekend. Mariah and I took the empty room next to the boy's room in the house. There was a twin bed in there for me to use, and just enough room to set up a crib for Mariah. I would be paid 150.00 a week along with room and board included, so it worked for me. Susan and I had become friends rather quick. We talked about everything under the sun, then the night came when we were talking in front of the fire place, all the kids were in bed. I started to feel comfortable enough with her that I could share my past with her. "I lived as a man for awhile." I told her. "I can see it." She was definitely intrigued by it, as I could feel myself slipping back towards the male role I could play so well.

The next morning, I was in the kitchen standing at the counter pondering over what to eat for breakfast. Susan came in and stood right beside me and said; "I could turn you on

just…like…. that!" She said while snapping her fingers. I thought I might collapse from her boldness. She was so sure of herself. "Really? we will see." I had told her. Now I was really starting to feel as I did before. I had managed to push aside all the feelings of wanting to be a man over the past year with making myself a total woman to the full extent, and even with that, women were going to be attracted to me still seeing the man hidden inside, once they knew my story.

After weeks of continuous flirtation between us, it was yet another night of couch conversations talking about what would have been if I had not flipped back and had remained on track to transitioning to a man. "Well, first off I would be a stuntman." That seemed to be my only regret at the time. I didn't want to be a stunt woman, and now with a child to take care of all bets were off on that kind of career. As the night went on, what had now turned into sexual tension grew. I felt "Marco" coming back and as that fire burned in the fireplace. it happened. We locked lips for a good long while before I realized this can't go any further as is. "I can't have sex with a woman as a woman, so this means I'm going to have to make a stop to the sex shop downtown." "What?" "Can't have sex without a dick, right"? She really didn't know what to say, and just the fact that she saw me as a man and not understanding why, was enough. She had said she had never been attracted to a woman before though now couldn't think of me as one anyway. I had to admit it made me feel pretty good. The next morning, I headed to the seedy part of town right to the sex shop that had been serving Riverside for many years. In fact, it was the only one I knew of.

It's always a bit nerve racking walking in to such an establishment, for me anyway.

I glanced around at all the different types of toys, many I wasn't sure what they were for exactly. I finally made my way to what are commonly known as dildos. What an odd word. I scanned the available merchandise on the shelf, always being drawn to the larger sized ones. Not anything over seven inches, but I wasn't interested in any small penis either. This time the purpose was only going to be for sex, not something I was going to keep in my pants for looks. No, this one would have to stay hidden in a drawer until needed, an on-call penis if you will. To relieve myself from embarrassment, I told the clerk at the register it was a gag gift for a friend, probably not believing me.

Driving back to Susan's house I began thinking how this was only about sex. I can't and will not have sex with a woman as a woman; and the fact that I now had a daughter; that made me her mother. I did everything in my power to suppress the feelings I had of needing to be a man, but the way I was going to actually have sex was going to have to be just as that, as a man, even though only mentally. One can wear many hats in the dark; our minds are a powerful tool at times. I had a high sex drive with or without testosterone injections, and during this time I felt desperate enough to have sex with whoever I could I suppose. I liked Susan very much as a friend, she made me laugh and we got along very well. I much rather would have liked her body to be a bit scaled down in size, but sometimes you have to take what you can get. It was different getting ready to become intimate with someone who already knows the truth, and is aware my penis is not flesh.

That did make things a bit more comfortable. That night once the kids were in bed, we did our usual couch chatting, which lead to the flirting she was so good at. It wasn't long before the kissing began, and she was a very good kisser. If a person could not kiss well, or conform to how I was kissing, it was over. Kissing is the very core of sensuality, it is what takes our minds to where they want to go. I think so anyway. Before I knew it, we were off to her bedroom to her giant-sized bed I swear you could sleep five in. The dark served its purpose for both of us. I never had to see really what she looked like without clothes on, and she never had to see what part I was missing, and those I wish I never had.

While she waited for me, I went to my secret drawer where the penis was hidden. In the darkness of the room, I slipped it into my underwear that was nowhere near big enough to accommodate the size. I made my way over to her bed and into her arms. I know she hadn't been laid in quite some time, nor was I so we both were ready for whatever this was going to be. I went right to climbing on top of her, both of us not able to get enough of each other with the kissing alone. I grabbed the tool inside my underwear, and eased it into her. Within just a few minutes we were both ready to come with all the thrusting for her and the rubbing from it for me, it was sexual bliss in the darkness where our minds could make it all be as real as we needed. After that, I slipped out of her bed and back to my room where Mariah slept in the quiet of the night.

After a few months of this Susan wanted it to be a permanent situation. She said; "What if I pay for your surgery?" Without hesitation I answered; I can't be Mariah's father, I am her mother. Even with an offer I never would have refused before, I simply felt I could not do such a thing to my child, even though she never would have known. I think my quick reaction stemmed from not foreseeing a longtime future with her for starters, and never wanted to be in that kind of debt to her I imagine. I was attempting to stay a woman as awkward as it was and having a child and going to church on a regular basis was what was keeping me on track. Or so I thought.

I was at the point where I felt I needed to get what I considered a real job. Susan was not even able to pay me anymore since she was in between nursing jobs only working twice a week. I ended up getting a job at Costco in Riverside. It paid pretty well, and for some reason was one of those places you can tell people you work at and is considered a primo place to work. After a couple of months working there, Mother's Day rolled around.

There was this guy that worked there I didn't really know much about. I was working at the door that day checking the customer receipts as they exited the store. I had noticed him out of the corner of my eye handing a rose every now and again to a woman. When he made his way over my way he said; "You're a mother aren't you?" Then he handed me a rose. I thanked him as he strode off. His name was Patrick, which suited him. The following week I was outside the store talking to a woman I had made friends with there about not dating anyone and it was not all that easy to find someone.

Patrick just happened to be walking by when I had said that, so for whatever reason I said out of jest to him; "Why don't you ask me out?" "Ok, will you go out with me"? He replied without hesitation. I was a little shocked since I wasn't serious, but I thought what would one date hurt? I wasn't attracted to him, and he was eleven years older than me, though the age gap does get smaller the older one becomes.

The thing is I felt as if I didn't belong in any category, as society puts everyone in to. That is until someone begins to bend the rules, or defy the norm. Those things are done on all different levels sometimes on purpose and sometimes not. For instance, from the time I was in junior high I deliberately made clothing decisions that were as far away from girls' clothes as my mother would allow me to go.

I was born with, at the very least, an oversized clitoris just by visual inspection. I came to understand this back in elementary school while in the basement at a friend's house. In comparison mine was twice the size of hers, as I could plainly see, so she thought it might be fun to apply clear coat nail polish to mine. Turns out that is not such a good idea as it began to burn terribly. I pulled my pants back up, bolted up the steps and out the garage door, running all the way home. I knew I had to tell my mom what happened.

With that she grabbed the receiver from the phone on the wall and called the girl's mom telling her what her daughter had done to me, making that the last time I ever visited her house. Was there more to the size of it? Medically I don't know, I never had any genetic testing done to find out whether I had battling chromosomes, however, I did learn about how in early fetal development that prenatal androgens have facilitative effects on male- typed activity including both child toy preferences and even when choosing a career later in life. Interesting information but does not answer the size question. Not saying that it always means that the individual will end up being transgendered, for a heterosexual female that would just be a typical tom-boy while growing up, which is what my mom was hoping for. All I did know is I felt out of place from the inside out and just kept waiting for me to change somehow so I would feel what is considered normal about one's self-identity.

A week or so before this encounter with Patrick, I had become very anxious over my living situation with Susan. I told her I needed to find my own place with my daughter. She didn't like the idea of me leaving, but I felt I needed to get away from her in the current capacity. I went looking unfortunately on the seedier side of Riverside near the downtown area, but not where the century old and probably haunted houses stood; big Victorian homes that had been turned into duplexes over the years. No, I had to settle for a tiny one bedroom apartment with a back door that lead right out to a dangerous alley where one night I heard gunshots right outside. I scooped up Mariah and went to hide in the tiled shower stall that was made of concrete. The cops came and we survived, but after that I knew our time there needed to be short. Since at the time it was what I could afford, I would have to make the best of it.

Susan and I discussed the reality of our relationship needing to be a nonphysical one, and we were able to remain friends. She was genuinely happy for me that I had a date with a guy on the weekend coming up. Since Susan would be babysitting for me that night, I had him pick me up from her house. Susan felt the need to make me look more womanly than normal, which entailed having to put up with her applying make-up to my face. I just kept thinking in my mind it was all for the best and tried to focus on the fact *I was a woman* and to accept it. This is the way it's supposed to be, find a nice guy to be with and move on through life like everyone else, and make my mom happy and proud. I can do this, I thought.

When Patrick arrived, he attempted to interact with Mariah, he sat and talked with both myself and Susan. He made good money, yet he drove an old Chevy Monza. It was embarrassing to be in since it had zero horsepower, really, zero. He said he was going to buy a truck soon, but for now that was it. We went to an Italian restaurant I remember I had a calzone. We talked about his ex-wife and how she spent all his money without him knowing until the bills came in. Isn't that always the case? If someone was spending all my money it wouldn't take me long to catch on. She had a daughter from a previous marriage, making him an instant stepfather. Apparently due to an MS diagnosis she became unable to conceive again. She also allegedly cheated on him for quite some time during the marriage, so he claimed, and finally had enough and divorced her.

After diner, we went to get Mariah and went back to my place. I ended up throwing up my food into the sink. Was it bad food? Or was I internally flipped out that I was attempting to date a guy. He didn't stay too much longer that night and not five minutes after he left my phone rang with calls from both Susan and Robin, wondering how the date went. I told them both he was very nice and even funny, but I was certainly not attracted to him. One day that week I went with Susan to Target and on the way over there she spoke of a really good-looking guy that was a cashier there. She said we would definitely go through his line so she could talk to him. Susan was such a flirt with her sultry voice, and clearly, she had a crush on him. As we approached his line Susan said, "My God he is so hot." I looked up at him as we moved closer, he had a great big smile on his face as we approached him with our cart full of stuff. He really was very good looking and very nice as well. Cashiers normally need to be in order to keep a job though. We ended up talking to him long enough for him to get the low down on where Susan lived in proximity to where he lived, which was fairly close to her. We ended up going to his place and meeting his wife who I expected to be gorgeous, this was not the case. She was very nice but very plain looking. They had a couple of kids together, and she had an older son from a previous marriage. His wife ended up becoming a babysitter for me while I was working at Costco.

A month later, Patrick flew back home to North Carolina where his family was for a visit. He left me with a firearm since I really was living in the ghetto. Before he left, I ended up having sex with him since that was what I needed to do to get used to being with a man. He spent the night, and that morning he said to me "So you used to be a man?" I nearly fell off the couch. How could he possibly know that? He mentioned that through the crack of the bathroom door he had seen me shaving a bit of my upper lip. If I recall correctly, there are many women who shave, or wax, or whatever it takes to remove facial hair that have never been on testosterone in their lives. For me, that was the reason for the continuing growth, though it was nowhere near enough for the makings of five o'clock shadow, it matters when you're not trying to present as a man. Even when the injections stop, the hair growth continues, but on a very small level. How did he know? He said it was intuition, like his mother apparently had, but I wasn't so sure. The important thing to me at the time is he never cared about my past.

While he was off visiting his family, the good-looking guy from Target, whose name was Josh, shows up at Costco knowing he would find me there. He came to tell me he wanted to speak to me in private.

He asked me to meet him at the park that is between his place and Susan's. I agreed, so I showed up that evening with Mariah, while he had his younger daughter with him. He told me he used to be into drugs and partied a lot and that was where he met who became his wife since she had become pregnant during those party days. He started telling me he was attracted to me and wanted to come by my place that night. Like the fool I was and based only on his looks, I agreed. I gave him the address and I felt like, wow, this guy is interested in me and he's hot.

By the time he got there Mariah was asleep, her second birthday was a few days away, and Patrick had left money to buy her something from him. It only took minutes from the time Josh walked through the door to my tiny place that we were pulling our clothes off each other working to get to the moment as fast as we could. I found myself very attracted to him. Who wouldn't be? I found myself wondering, for a moment, am I transgendered or not? Have I just not ever been completely attracted to a guy before or what? I knew that was not really the case. I had been, I just never wanted to have sex with any of them since I had always felt I was on the wrong side of that equation, but now I was trying to be what I knew I was not, just mushing forward with blinders on. I would remain obsessed with the penis, from an envy standpoint. Before we knew it, we were having sex right there on the living room floor. Not once, but twice.

As attractive as he was, and as incredibly satisfying was the moment, I knew it could not happen again. Not because either of us would object to making it an on going fling, but he had a family himself, while I still continued to shield those thoughts of the man inside I was fighting to suppress. I wasn't confused, I was running away from my true self, which is not an easy thing to do… trust me. Obviously, I didn't feel a thing for Patrick since I took this sexual opportunity without even a moment of hesitation. At this point in my life, I needed security for my daughter, she was the only thing keeping me from flipping my brain right back to before *the voice* in my car.

Less than twenty-four hours later, Josh started showing up at my work, day after day telling me he was in love with me and was going to leave his wife and children for me, pleading with me to just give us a chance. I told him that was crazy; we hardly know each other outside of twenty minutes of pleasure, and here I was thinking I was the impulsive one. The next day was Mariah's birthday that I needed to prepare for. I bought her a Little Tykes orange and blue slide with the money Patrick left for her gift, along with a stuffed Barney the dinosaur who unfortunately was very popular at the time with toddlers.

Even though where we lived at the time was a less desirable area, it did have a very quaint back yard with a big shady oak tree where the party was held. Just a few friends with their kids, Josh had come bringing along his wife, daughters and step son. I didn't feel awkward myself; I made it a point not to. Susan and her two sons were there as well. Overall it was a nice day for Mariah, though she will never remember it.

When Patrick returned from North Carolina, we discussed the danger of living where I did with my two year old child. He himself was renting a small house that belonged to a long time friend of his that was out of state for an extended period of time. He asked me if I wanted to move in. I immediately agreed mainly because it would be free rent, and for the most part Patrick and I got along well. As true as that was, he seemed to lack the dangers of safety hazards around a toddler. Leaving buck knives on the dining room table within Mariah's reach was becoming quite annoying. Was this a possible red flag?

Absolutely.

We spent one Christmas in that house, with me buying too many gifts for Mariah. My own memories of Christmas as a child clouded the reality that children at a very young age, not only don't understand what it is all about, but could care less on the amount of stuff they receive. My mom started the Christmas shopping in the late summer. She was smart for sure. When Santa Claus ceased to exist, me and my older brother, Nick found the hiding place to the enormous number of toys that were being stashed for the special day, in the closet of the playroom downstairs. Nick said to me one evening "Let's go take a peek at our presents." I followed him to the secret door, standing behind him as he started to open it where all the treasure was. "No, I can't look, I want to be surprised!"

I left him there alone if he felt he needed to cheat. We normally got everything we asked for, which was always circled in the *Sears Christmas catalog*. I still remember waiting impatiently for that magical book to arrive in our mailbox. That feeling never really goes away, does it?

Still forcing myself down what was considered the right path in life, the most logical thing to do was to marry this person that cared so much about me, accepted me for who I was, and now I was pregnant with his first child. Patrick proposed to me, which I can hardly remember any of that now, but I did say yes. Why? Good question. I called my mom, she was ecstatic, all the more reason to do it. Very quickly the wedding was planned, invitations went out, and the date was set for February 8th, 1994. The eighth will come up again, but that will come much later. My mother in tow with two of her sisters and one of my cousins flew in from Illinois for this big event in Las Vegas. My friend Kenzie was there as well. The first time she could get me alone that day she had only one question to ask me. "Are you sure you want to do this?" I told her yes, but I believe she knew better. She knows me better than anyone possibly could, even through years of little communication.

I was just throwing myself into a family life that I was convinced would make everything better, make *me* better. Having to wear a dress for this occasion was a very unsettling feeling for me, as soon as it was over, and all photos were taken, I tore it off, and replaced it with a loose button-down shirt, shorts, and hiking boots, which my mother detested.

I felt good that day because I made her happy. There were so many years I felt like I caused her so much pain, that I had to make up for it somehow. I wish I could have come up with something different, that's for sure. If you only take away one remaining thought from reading this; let it be to never do something totally drastic in your life just to please someone else. It will backfire somewhere down the line.

The next big change was going to be to Montana. The Costco location in Riverside was closing despite the hundreds of signatures from residents they would prefer it to stay open, and not be turned it into a skating rink. This meant the employees were to disperse to other locations or take a severance. I took the money naturally, and Patrick was offered a company move to Missoula, Montana. We decided to take it and run. We both wanted to get away from California, and I guess I felt like maybe I could put more distance between my transgender past. My only focus was on Mariah and this new baby that was going to be here soon. What Montana does have going for it is beauty, that cannot be argued. The drive there alone proved to be taxing for me on a parental level. The heater of all things went out on my 1972 Chevy Chevelle I was allowing him drive. There sat Mariah in the back, in her car seat, bundled and wrapped like a mummy so she would not freeze.

I was furious and continued to complain for several miles until we stopped so I could buy her some gloves. When we reached the frozen tundra in late March, we stayed with complete strangers who worked for Costco there for a few days until we found a place to live. They were very nice people, easy enough to get along with. We rented the other side of a duplex owned by the other tenant. Her father owned a car dealership in town.

The hospital was literary a two minute drive, and on August 22nd 1994 there I was for the second time telling a nurse to grab a blue blanket for the birth of my child. This time it did not go as quickly as the first time, this child must be stubborn I thought. Walking halls and them having to break my water seemed like a lot of work. I pondered the child's name as I watched the news that day on the T.V. in the room. I told Patrick if it were to be a girl, though that seemed impossible to me…I already had one…but the name could not be what we had already agreed on. I didn't like Brianna Ashton anymore. Within the next hour Madison Taylor Davis was born, and the blue blanket remained although it was a girl, which is totally fine. Who likes pink anyway? Patrick cut her cord and it seemed he began to bond with the tiny person that was his first child. Madison was a handful, she hated to ride in the car for any period of time, and her sleep pattern was reversed so she was up in the night and slept in the day. Two months into her life, Patrick had a revelation one day while showering, that he felt he had to return to North Carolina to his parents' house. It didn't matter to me that we left Missoula, as beautiful a landscape it is, I wasn't hooked to living in such a small community. Blindly we left for the Eastern Coast without jobs waiting for either of us.

When Madison was six months old it was discovered by a nurse practitioner that one of her legs was shorter than the other. I figured she would just have to wear one of those chunky soled shoes on one foot and move on with life. The outcome of x-rays revealed she was born with hip dysplasia. Viewing such an x-ray anyone can clearly see that the ball joint on one side is up higher than the other. She was immediately placed in a metal brace with cuffs that clamped on both legs with a bar running through the middle connecting both sides. She had to wear it 23 hours a day. It only came off at bath time. Madison was a very determined baby; she learned to crawl in that thing. Even up a big flight of stairs back then. After months of mandatory brace wearing, it began to improve slightly, but due to her own physical growth she now needed a larger one. She hated wearing it by this time and the last time I tried to put it on her I couldn't do it to her. She was eighteen months old and I just couldn't upset her anymore at that point. I left it off and just prayed it would heal the rest of the way on its own. It did, praise God.

FOURTEEN

*I*t had been thirteen years since Patrick and his two sisters, along with their parents, had all spent the holidays together. Upon our arrival his mother could not have been happier to be with her son's first child, as she scooped Madison from his arms. They lived in a house on the lake in a very small rural town called Creswell, population 400. The closest Walmart was forty-five minutes away. His mother didn't really care for me; she had indicated to Patrick early on after our wedding that she felt he had married a man. I was not offended by that in any way, and only proved her keen perception.

At the time Mariah was three, and like most three-year-olds she liked to pick up things and put them in her little backpack. When Patrick's sixteen-year-old niece had not been able to find one of her Gameboy games, and then it was discovered in Mariah's backpack, Patrick's mother blew a gasket and called Mariah a thief. I yelled back at her stating the fact that she was only three. It got pretty ugly, and I was done with staying there at that point. We both had found jobs, and a place to rent relatively quick. Though we hardly made it financially it was worth it to not feel so scrutinized.

Patrick was off in Raleigh at some training class for work when I got the call from one of his sisters that their mother had died in the night. I called him not really able to break it to him; he thought there was something wrong with the next baby that was to be born. "Your mom died last night." All he said was, "I will be there as fast as I can get there." He was very close to his mom as was his sister Nancy. Their mother was the glue of that family; things would never be the same for any of them. Patrick's dad liked me, I liked him too. The property they lived on was pretty big, he had a little convenience store on the grounds for the guys that would fish in the lake that the house sat on. He offered shelves of collectable baseball cards by the box for sale, along with snacks, drinks and other neat little things. There was even a pool table in the back room.

The only problem living in such a rural place is you're going to be poor unless you have your own lucrative business, or you work for the state. At the beginning of our peak in poverty, Jennifer Rachel Davis was born on September 18th 1995 only thirteen months after Madison. What the hell was I thinking? That was the problem. I wasn't, I just kept pushing myself further away from my mental reality. Not for one second did I not love my kids; I just never should have had them. That was not my plan, and to this day I question myself about that day in the car when I heard; "Do you know who you are?" And instantaneously I changed back. Why? I cannot answer that. I didn't want to. All I can say now it was meant to be, they were meant to be born, and I love them all.

Before Jennifer was born, I desperately wanted to get out of the marriage. I called the guy I worked for when I used to throw newspapers in Riverside to see if he would give me a job. He said sure, there always seemed to be a route coming up needing to be thrown.

What the hell was I going to do with two little kids and one on the way? I knew I was not being realistic at that point. I was just starting to unravel inside my mind. My kids were the only thing keeping me from coming completely unglued. I knew I made a mistake marrying anyone at that time in my life. Again, it was to make other people happy. Even worse on my part was this last conception was on purpose, in reality they all were. I continued thinking I could make everything alright as long as we kept having kids, somehow it would make me become the gender in which I was born physically. We could not have been worse off financially at the time. We ended up on food stamps to feed the kids. Our truck was repossessed in the middle of the night, the very one my mother paid to have the transmission rebuilt, and brought the loan back up to current status only to have it taken away.

We ended up hanging up the towel in North Carolina and thought we would actually try living in my home town. Once again it was my mother to the rescue, when she sent us three thousand dollars to buy a late eighties Ford mini-van Eddie Bauer edition, making it slightly sporty; to get us to Illinois. Jennifer was still a new baby and it was winter now, with Illinois being a very cold place that time of year. We briefly stayed with my mom.

Her house had a whole finished basement, with a bedroom as well, so there was plenty of room. We scoured the want ads for jobs and a place to live. As usual Patrick ventured far off from the beaten path to find work.

He ended up at a Sam's Club fifty-six miles away, and I at the very retail building I grew up near and was grounded at the age of five because me and my only friend at the time, Tiffany, decided we wanted to go there. It was a wonderful fall day as we walked up our street, around the corner and to the dead end, then crossing the empty field until you hit the slope of concrete that morphed into a giant parking lot. There it was, Masons department store. We entered the enormous building and only went as far as the sea of candy and toy machines that lined both sides of the enclosed entrance. We were so mesmerized by all the choices we had to spend our nickels and dimes on, we had lost track of all real time. What five-year-old and six-year-old wouldn't?" As we walked out one of the sets of double doors to begin our journey home, Tiffany's mother rolled up in their 1967 Ford Fairlane. My heart dropped. She was pissed off for sure. I barely remember the one and a half minute's ride home, besides the slick black leather back seat we both sat quietly on. But as soon as I hit the back door to our house, I was toast. My mother brought me down to the basement and set me in the yellow chair with the steps that came out if you wanted them to, I loved that chair come to think of it. She confiscated the purple patch with blue lettering I had purchased with my dime that said; "Be mine." She warned me of the strangers that could have taken me away, and then sent me to my room for the rest of the day.

Masons had not been Masons in years, and by the time I was employed there, it was ValuCity. I figured working in my home town that I surely would see people I knew. But nothing could have prepared me for being stopped in my tracks at the same time as Jana was stopped in hers when our eyes met. I thought I might throw up. Both of us were speechless, I wanted to say something but nothing would come out. Then I noticed her look of anger and hate, which left nothing to say. I don't think I will ever get over that moment. My mind was pulled in two different directions. One was back to when we were teenagers in love as I acted out the role of the boy trapped desperately inside a female body. The other processing thought was I am a woman, I have kids now, can we just be friends and call it a day? That was most certainly an impossibility.

As hard as I tried to be what society viewed me as, I only found myself standing there wishing I really was a man so I could walk over to her and hold her forever in my arms, since my mind still refused to let go of what was once between us. I have only recently learned that she is now aware that I am physically who I was only mentally back when we could never get enough of each other, but she had made it clear to the inquirer who was Margot over the phone that she had no desire of communicating with me on any level, ever. I have to wonder if she at least was curious enough to look me up on Facebook.

As nice as it was to be staying with my mom so she could spend time with her grandchildren, it was also a reminder of just how bizarre she could be. In our short stay with her, she went from the gracious hostess she could be, to despising the fact that we were taking up any kind of space in her home. She became bitter and cruel, throwing us out. This was how it was growing up under her roof, though nothing swayed my love for her, I knew I couldn't stay around her too long allowing her to hurt me even more. We ended up finding a house to rent within that week, naturally on borrowed money. That lasted about six months only to have us going back yet again to North Carolina. We were always running. My hometown of Ottawa, Illinois was not the same.I was not the same. I didn't feel it would ever be the place I could stay the rest of my life. In that part of the country many people do live and die in the same town still. It was a great place to grow up in the seventies and eighties, but my vision, especially my deep seated one, would never be able to unfold there. I will always miss it, but that's common enough, missing the place you come from. John Cougar Mellencamp got it right in his "Small Town" song with the line *I cannot forget where it is I come from*. It's true, we don't.

When we arrived back in North Carolina, we stayed a few days with Patrick's sister Nancy while we searched for a place to live. Again, ending up in Creswell the same tiny and dead-end place we were before. There I was still figuring I needed to be the woman and mother I clearly was. Or so I continued to make myself believe. Now, since I was stuck being a woman, I felt I still needed a son, someone who was a part of me…and a boy. These were the crazy thoughts I had with the notion to make them true. Both Patrick and I were working full time jobs driving a good distance to get to them since that's the way it is in that part of North Carolina. Did I mention rural? This went on for months, barley getting by as usual. I hated my life, but loved my kids. I felt I was stuck for sure with my gender now; I had kids, and I was that word I just could not identify within my mind, "Mother." Yes, that was the one. I began to feel even more now, at this point, I needed to have a son. I must have felt I might somehow live through him since I was not a man myself.

On July 15th, 1997, Jonathan Patrick Davis was born. We knew five months prior to his birth he was a boy, bringing sheer joy for the both of us. The day he was born quickly became alarming. He, unlike his sisters didn't cry upon entering this world, not a peep. It took me a bit to realize something wasn't right. They swept him away immediately as I watched a nurse go to the phone and call a doctor in. Within thirty seconds he appeared and stood over Jonathan working on him while three other nurses attended. He was born with a collapsed lung. They needed to inflate it and stabilize him in order to transfer him to the Children's Hospital in Raleigh. It was right across the street from The Ronald McDonald House which I was already familiar with when Madison had gone through her days of running tests when she was diagnosed with hip dysplasia. It took three hours to get him to the point where he could be transported by ambulance. While we waited in my room, a nurse finally brought him to us just to see him, not able to touch him before he would be on his way. It was very hard to watch him leave.

I was home the next day packing a bag to go stay near him for the next week. He was in the neonatal unit, and was the biggest baby there. My God I had never seen a baby under four pounds before. There were several in there. After alerting my mom about Jonathan's situation she began a prayer chain among her friends and beyond. Within twenty-four hours he improved quicker than any baby ever had in that unit. My biggest concern then became him getting circumcised. I was frantic with the idea it would not get done. Every day for seven days I reminded the nurse on duty to be sure it was done before we left. It was the last thing, on the seventh day that was done before I took him home. Just as the time before, life in North Carolina proved to not be profitable.

We had already decided we would return to California after Jonathan's birth. We drove back when he was six weeks old, we ended up renting a small three-bedroom townhome in not one of the better neighborhoods in Riverside. The Complex was nice enough, it was just how close we were to some of the drug dealing activity that went on around us. This place had been vacant for awhile, which was obvious with the incredible amount of overgrown weeds in the small enclosed back area considered a yard. The owner agreed to take one hundred dollars off the cost of moving in if we cleaned it up ourselves. It was early September and still hot outside as it normally is in Southern California. As I was dripping with sweat while I continued to eradicate the small jungle, I noticed in my peripheral a tall black dude peering over the dog-eared fence that separated our tiny back yards. "Do you want something to drink?" He asked, while I had also spotted a tiny face resembling Vanessa Williams at the age of seven also peering through the fence at me. "Ok, sure." He had gone inside and came back out with a bottle of water for me. "Thanks." I said as he handed it to me over the fence. He seemed like a nice enough guy I thought, and had at least a daughter I could see, that was around Mariah's age.

After about a week, a blonde headed woman emerged from next door. I watched her walk down the sidewalk with a baby in a carrier. She must be that guy's wife I thought, and the mother of the little girl I saw the week before. It wasn't long before Mariah had become friends with not only the Vanessa Williams look alike, there was also another girl in between the oldest and the youngest. They began to play outside, and going in and out of each other's homes. I finally met the blonde haired slightly overweight woman by default since our kids became friends. She was very nice, took her kids to church as I was taking my own. She worked for a high school as a security guard and was also their swim coach. At the time, I was throwing newspapers in the early morning hours so I could always be home with my kids. We got along very well, spending a good amount of time at the pool until it became too cold to swim. She had taught Jennifer to swim at the age of three, back when Jenny was fearless doing front flips into the pool. Something I had to put a stop to when she narrowly escaped cracking her head open on the edge upon entry.

Over the months of conversation, we got to know one another pretty well. I ended up telling her of my past; how I had lived as a man for awhile several years ago and believing it was God that turned me back to staying a woman. She certainly didn't seem surprised, and had no problem with the facts of my story. These were the kinds of testimonies born again Christians' revel upon. I just had to keep believing in my mind that I was doing the right thing by God and that in time everything would fall in to place. Things between Patrick and me in the bedroom were odd. It was true I didn't ever want to have sex being on the female side of the equation, I always preferred oral for several reasons. Even as a woman I didn't think of oral sex being all that intimate, same as most guys feel about getting a blow job. Body image is everything. The fact that I hated mine inside and out didn't help matters much.

After one too many nights of my waking up in the very late hours and seeing Patrick in the glow of the computer monitor's screen he was sitting in front of, made me wonder why he was up so late, so often. That morning when he left, I did a little detective work. I found a floppy disc with naked photos of a woman, and a note pad he had been feverishly writing what I saw to be sexual things he wanted to do to her. The words unfolded before my eyes when I shaded across the paper indentations left behind, with a pencil, on the page that had been underneath the page on which he was writing the night before and had removed. At first, I was incredibly hurt. I just didn't get it. I had a decent body even though I didn't like the biological makeup of it. I would have understood somewhat if I were a fat cow or something. I was pretty upset over it, I felt betrayed.

I ran next door to the blonde and cried on her shoulder. She comforted me, she cared about me. When Patrick got home from work, I confronted him, he did nothing but try to deny the floppy disc as his, and dance around the subject at hand. I told him to pack his bags and get out. He began the task of packing while he sulked, and proceeded to tell the kids I was kicking him out. Naturally they didn't understand and wanted him to stay.

That was the beginning of the end for me.

The day of my birthday, six months after we had lived there, the blonde asked me out to dinner that night, and I accepted. We went and had a good time, then when we were driving back, she asked if we could go park somewhere to talk instead of going home. I drove past our street and on to the baseball diamond's parking lot and parked my car.

Right in the middle of one of my sentences she moved in quick and kissed me on the mouth. I kind of pushed her back just a little since I was so caught off guard. "I love you." Just flew out of her mouth. "What? you can't possibly." I had told her. "But I do, and want to be with you." "Look, like I said before, I can't be with a woman as a woman, we need to get back home now." I said as I started the car up and drove off. In my mind at that very moment things began to become very clear, the things I had been hiding and ignoring over the last several years since I heard *the voice* in the car. It didn't matter how much I tried to be a woman, even all the way to giving actual birth which was never ever in my plans of life prior to *the voice*.

FIFTEEN

*N*ow that I realized what was still happening despite my efforts to fight it off, things began to change. My mind was now slowly shifting back to before *the voice*. The blonde was head over heels in love with me, and as slightly creepy as that was at first, I ran with it. She could make me feel like the man I knew I was; still trapped inside. I started to gradually blend my wardrobe back more to the male spectrum, not that it had very far to go anyway. I was spending everyday with the blonde; she started running everyday for weeks achieving a forty pound weight loss. She wanted to look better for me, I knew since now she cared what she looked like.

She was in a marriage she threw herself into for the wrong reasons, as so many people do. We snuck out whenever we could driving one of our cars anywhere we thought we could go and make out for awhile. With every passing day I began to feel more and more trapped within myself. I felt there was no way out, and I started feeling like I was living a double life, in my head anyway. I found it harder to tolerate Patrick's passive aggressive behavior and needed to get away from him and figured this might be a good time to drive up North with the blonde to visit Tita my birthmother, who I met in person the year before. That was interesting to say the least, as I was totally unprepared for what reality can be when your birthmother opens the door for the first time. All I had to go on was a twenty-year-old photo of her, on the cover of a 48-page book of poems she had sent me, which I did appreciate.

Tita was living in the bottom half of a two-story home in San Francisco rent free with a monthly salary in exchange for giving 24-hour care to an elderly Italian woman. It was a good situation for her to be in since it seemed for several years, she was unable to hold down any kind of regular job, actually she refused to. Her own family outside of one brother shunned her for the most part, they couldn't understand her refusal to conform to the norm at that time, and my unexpected, and unbelievable conception made matters even worse. She is certainly an odd bird, but at the time it was still early in my meetings with her and wanted to make the effort to build some kind of relationship.

When we arrived in San Francisco, being only my second visit, it was my first time experiencing driving the streets looking for an address. One thing is for sure, I personally would never want to drive a stick on a daily basis in this city. We reached the home and pulled over to park in front. I called Tita to let her know we had made it. She told me to have us walk down the steps on the side of the house that lead to the backside of the property and into the bottom part of the house where she was living. It was a very quaint backyard with flowers growing everywhere, with a small private garden. Tita had come out the door and down the few concrete steps to meet us in the yard.

She then hugged me, and asked me if I was "with" the blonde. I told her yes. To her it was really not a big deal being she considered herself bi-sexual, and she just wasn't one to judge. We went inside to find a studio apartment set up. A small kitchen straight ahead, with a living room off to the left as you walked in. There was a bathroom off of that room, then steps leading to the upstairs where the old Italian woman lived, and always waited for Tita. She told us they would talk for hours in Italian, that was the main reason Tita was hired by the daughter of this woman. She was paid cash naturally, and was able to save nearly every dime in the year and a half she was employed by the family.

She led both of us over to a small love seat and told us to sit. She then stood right in front of me while reaching down to cup my face in both her hands and said; "My beautiful boy." I certainly was not offended by the comment in any way, but the fact that she had said it not knowing of my hidden self was quite strange to me. Her living space had no extra room for the blonde and me to spend the night, so we drove to my birth father's apartment where he offered us a pull-out couch to sleep that night. Now he on the other hand was the complete polar opposite of Tita. On any given day these two people would never have come together as a perfect fit as a couple, not even a little bit. This brings me to the bizarre but true story of how I even came to be.

My birth father was stationed in Livorno, Italy when he was in the Army. He met a girl there and fell in love. This girl was Tita's older sister. Tita was only eleven at the time, and she tells the story of how my birth father had saved her from drowning once. When the time came for him to leave Italy, he asked the girl to come with him back to the United States and marry him. They returned to his hometown of Denver Colorado.

They bought a house and started a family. After having two boys, both young; Tita's sister had become pregnant a third time. She thought it might be a good idea for her now older little sister to come and live with them in the United States, not only to help out with the kids, but figured there would be more opportunities for her than in Italy. Not to mention their father was a tyrant and she was glad to get away from him. Tita hopped a plane to Denver when she was nineteen without knowing one bit of English.

It seemed that the stress of a third pregnancy was too much on Tita's sister and the marriage had become strained in the bedroom. My birth father found Tita quite attractive seven years later and all grown up. The evening of the birth of their third child was the night I was conceived. Back then in 1964 the father didn't accompany their wife in the delivery room. The father of a child would wait for the news of the birth, then go home and let them both rest a couple of days before bringing them home. He had received a call while at work when his wife went into labor, then went home to take her to the hospital. He waited there until the birth of who I now know to be my half-sister. At that point he would have gone home until the call would come that they were both ready to be picked up.

It was evening by then, he came in to find both his boys already asleep in their room and Tita sitting on the floor watching T.V., he now had a plan. He went to take a shower then joined her on the floor gazing up at the flickering television for a few moments, he then proceeded to fling his robe open exposing his semi erect large penis. This prompted Tita to touch it, and give it a few hard tugs, but only for a few seconds according to her. I myself can now attest that is all it takes if the mood is right. He tried to continue to take things further as he got up and grabbed her by the hand, leading her to his and her sister's bedroom. When they reached the room he let his robe drop to the floor, then told her to take off her clothes. She did as he said, then as he began to move towards her with what she describes and the biggest penis she had ever seen, she stopped him and said, "I cant do this to my sister." As she proceeded to gather her nightshirt, her underwear were accidently left behind. She then went in to the boys room where they were still asleep. She laid down on her side facing the wall on the spare twin bed that was provided for her to sleep. Moments later he came to the room and laid right behind her spooning her as he said, "Where can I put it?" She stayed motionless, and didn't say a word, with her eyes shut tight she only hoped he would just go away. Without him hearing an answer from Tita, she began to feel him rhythmically force his penis between her thighs while he finished himself off. Now, there seems to be a missing part to this since my conception took place at all. I had tried to get the blank filled in by both of them asking them precisely about penetration. They both said on separate occasions there was none. Sperm has been known to travel, though this trip was a long one.

When she wound up pregnant, they both were totally astounded. She uses the word rape, he says it was mutual, but they both agree there was no penetration. Now let's consider that word. The fact that they didn't ride out the night in sexual bliss accounts for their stories being truthful. Once the word was out to the immediate family members, excluding their parents back in Italy, Tita was shunned. She was immediately sent to her oldest sister in Illinois to be taken to Peoria, Illinois to an unwed mothers home run by Catholic Social Services. This sister was the one who told Tita to go across the border to Mexico to get an abortion since they were not legal in US at the time. She refused as much as she didn't want a baby at the given time, she wasn't comfortable with killing it, well actually killing me.

Upon arrival, Tita was sat down in an office with papers before her on a desk. Papers to sign away her rights as the mother of the child she carried. She signed because this is what she was told to do, but at the same time she didn't ask to become a mother. Seven months later on March 24th 1965, I was born at St Francis Hospital in Peoria, Illinois. She was only allowed to hold me for a few moments, just enough time to count all my fingers and toes. She called her oldest sister and told her how beautiful I was, and how blue my eyes were. Her sister's response was, "Do not even think about walking out of the hospital with that baby." She was a disgrace to the family; I was nothing to any of them and she had no support.

Twelve years would pass before Tita would tell her parents she had given birth. In September of 1964 my, to-be, parents were told that there would be a baby available in March, so they signed the papers to take me six months before I was born. Tita has told me that eight months later she drove back to Illinois to Catholic Social Services to see about getting me back. They told her I was in an orphanage. They lied. She attempted again in 1983 to find me through Catholic Social Services but during that time all documents were still sealed. She had actually been upset with me that I didn't make the same effort as she did. I personally was afraid of rejection, and still am to this day.

Bringing things back to the pull-out couch. I'm sure me and the blonde one messed around that night though I can't recall to what level. What I do remember is we ended up drifting apart on the trip home. We spent one night in a beachside hotel since we had the reservation, not to mention it's almost a seven-hour drive back to Riverside. She wanted to jump in bed and get to it. I didn't want to, so that naturally caused problems throughout the night. When I woke the next morning, she was not in the room. I looked out the window and saw her walking on the beach. I went down to catch up with her finding she really didn't want to talk. "What do you want me to say?" I asked her, it's not you, it's me." I told her. "I don't get you; you bring me here, and then want nothing to do with me physically." She responded. "Here is the thing, I am a woman as wrong as that feels, and as painful is that is for me to even say, I also have four kids I need to raise."

"And again, I'm not going to be in any relationship with a woman as one, that's just not a possibility for me, I'm not a lesbian; if only it were that simple, we wouldn't be having this conversation now would we." I found myself very irritated that I had to even mention that again. She only stood there and stared at me as I told her we just needed to get back home. The long ride home was silent outside of the radio playing as the pavement became never-ending. When we finally reached home there were no words said. She went through her back gate, as I went through mine. As my behavior continued to sway with every passing day, I knew in my mind that one day I would not be able to continue living a life as something I could not identify with on a level of acceptance to myself. I was utterly lost and broken.

Me and the blonde one continued to have an on again, off again sexual relationship depending when my male side was overwhelming. It had finally become apparent to Patrick that something really was going on between her and I. The last time I had spent the night with her was when we had gone to see a Doobie Brothers show at a dinner theatre. I was in full male swing that night. I bought the tickets, drove us there in the pouring rain, pulled her as close to me as possible without being detected in such a way. This was because I did not want to be thought of as a lesbian couple naturally. They put on quite a good show by the way, they sounded just as they did thirty years before. It was a fun night and I certainly expected to get laid after all that. It never happened, she didn't want to, and her kids were downstairs, and blah, blah, blah.

When Patrick had gotten up the next morning and saw I wasn't there, he came next door and started pounding on her door knowing I was inside. He was all pissed off telling her that she was not going to take me from him, I told him he was nuts. At this point I knew I had to get out of what was the biggest mistake of my life, this marriage I was in, that should never have taken place. Over the next few months, me and the blonde spent quite a bit of time together, ducking out behind closed doors at the drop of a hat; as I would slam her up against a wall to make out if only for a few moments. As good as the passion felt, I again was not feeling right about it since in reality I still had the wrong body parts. It beame mentally debilitating at times if I was not able to refocus on another thought.

She had her own demons about our relationship as well. While we were together, she decided to start dating another guy at the same time. I didn't get it, and wasn't really all that bothered by it, wondering if she was only trying to make me jealous.

The day came where I ended the relationship; that devastated her for some reason. I was shocked by her broken behavior, when she burst out into uncontrollable tears as she slid down the wall into a fetal position. It was also becoming quite clear to me that I couldn't keep being something I was not on the inside. My reality was all too real, though I knew it would still be a while before I could do anything about it. The following year as hard as I guess I tried to remain friends with the blonde, she ended up getting crazy on me when she decided to key my 1989 Camaro SS. That was painful.

We stopped speaking all together, also, we as a family bought a house up in Apple Valley and moved out of the area. I continued to try to be a mother to my children. I was, but always felt out of place. Especially when I would get a "Mother and daughter tea" invite. I would cringe while reading such a thing. I know that sounds terrible, but I just never fit the mold of what a mother was supposed to act like. Believe me, my kids knew that too. They were not bothered by the way I acted, or even how I looked compared to other kids' moms, at least not to my knowledge. There were times when my temper would get out of control. I never hit my children, but I could be very scary nonetheless. The anger I held inside over the way I really felt, hating the fact I was a woman, and continued in a marriage that I had horribly regretted could easily set me off. The memory is nearly lost in my mind, only remembering that after a phone call I had received had enraged me enough to grab and throw a yellow two -pound ceramic dinner plate like a Frisbee full force down the hallway towards the back wall, where all the kids' bedrooms were situated on both sides. When Jennifer opened her and Madison's door the plate sailed right past her face nearly missing her as it slammed into the wall breaking into several pieces scattering about on the tile floor.

It seemed like a good idea moving away from the things that hindered me in my quest to be a mother and wife. Two words that I still can't fathom I ever was, but that didn't change how my brain operated as a male trapped inside an unwanted female body. I immersed myself in the renovation of the house to my own liking, tearing out mauve colored carpet and replacing it with tile, then painting every room a different color. It was therapy for me. Eventually we would build a room addition that became Mariah's bigger bedroom. My other deep dive was staying focused on Mariah's apparent volleyball skills she had discovered while still in Riverside at the age of eight. She was now ten, and was playing club volleyball. I was certainly proud of her, being a more skilled player than most of the then thirteen year olds. Lots of time and money goes along with this kind of thing. There are crucial tryouts, believe me, this is definitely not Parks and Rec. I was an athlete, so I only felt it was natural that my children would all be as well. Mariah was the only one to be. I ended up living vicariously through her success with this sport for a total of seven years, keeping myself busy with the kind of dedication that goes along at playing at such a level. This kept my mind off of what I was, that I had hidden from myself for so long, pretending that it wasn't real. Focus on what is real at this time, I told myself. Which was Mariah's success.

The most memorable game of all those years was when she was twelve, and her team was down by thirteen points. When they got the ball back it was her turn to serve; overhand just to clarify. Every single one of her serves was like a bullet; not one of the opponents could even begin to get underneath any of her serves making those thirteen aces in a row to win that game and end the match. The entire crowd went wild! pouring out of the bleachers to the floor towards her, with me leading the pack. When I reached her I picked her up and said "this is my kid!" Even now tears roll reliving that proud moment.

We had probably lived in the house for a little over a year when my cousin Diane had called me to let me know my mom had been in the hospital and that she could not be alone anymore. Diane had been staying the night in the spare bedroom and was being paid to do so. My mother now needed to be driven around town for her what now became consistent doctor's appointments and her usual errands. She would now be on oxygen 24/7. I knew that day would come, she started smoking at eighteen, and was now sixty- eight. She called me when she was up to it, and I told her I still did not want her in a convalescent home. We had that conversation years before and I told her she would live with me.

Now that time had come. I flew home in August 2001, a month before 9/11, and brought my mom back with me to California in October 2001, a month after 9/11. That was sheer stress as I recall at the time. One of my last memories of being with my mom was at take off from Chicago, holding her hand and telling her that if anything happened on that flight, and it was going to go down, I personally was not going to let it happen without a fight. That was the Nation's view on all that at the time.

It was very hard on her to have to leave, but we both knew my brother was not going to take care of her. After she left Illinois there was an estate sale, which I was not a part of, and then the sale of her house. There were so many things I now wish I had that now belong to strangers. The older I get the more I appreciate vintage items. I always had liked old things, but you just start to realize the value more as time goes by. Many times, not the monetary value, most are sentimental, just the memory of something from a certain time in our lives that always takes us back to that feeling connected with an item.

Upon arrival to California flying in to LAX, there was a problem. My mom's oxygen tank had run seriously low by the time we got into the terminal. Her breathing became labored, and our ride was late, which was Susan. Finally, I saw her flinging her arms at us. I told her what was going on and she immediately grabbed a random airport attendant and told them to call 911. The paramedics were there within minutes. They gave her more oxygen, leaving enough with her for us to get home. Prior to her coming I had to set up a home service of oxygen delivery. This consists of an oxygen concentrator that is plugged into the wall with a constant flow of oxygen through tubing running into the patient's nostrils. Also, enough small portable canister tanks to take along wherever the patient needs to go outside the home.

It's a sad picture for sure. She had been diagnosed with emphysema eleven years prior to the state she was now in. I don't really remember her actually trying to quit smoking, though I remember trying to talk to her about it when I was a teen. She said she was too nervous to quit, and now she only had one quarter of her lung capacity left. I remember when I explained that to my kids at the time, they were all pretty young, so I drew a picture of a pie and cut it in four equal parts. Then I shaded in only one quarter of the pie. I told them that was the only part left for grandma to breathe.

Now my kids are nineteen years older, as am I come to think of it, time really does fly. I never thought any of them would ever smoke watching my mom needing aide to breathe with oxygen attached to her face. Madison however decided to take up smoking pot, which I have always detested. She introduced both her brother Jonathan and sister Jennifer to it as well so the three of them had, in my book, become pot heads. Mildly maybe but still they smoked it. Madison also picked up the habit of smoking just regular cigarettes as well, for a shot time. That was awhile ago now, all of them are in different places in life, not smoking anymore. For those of us who don't smoke anything wonder how the people that do can ignore the very possible outcome in the end. I used to enjoy the reality of the American Cancer Society's horrific commercials of real people gasping for breath while covering their tracheotomy hole with their finger trying to talk, or showering, or even simply trying to breathe at all even while connected to their oxygen tanks.

Upon my mother's arrival to our home things were fine in the beginning I suppose. The adjustment for her was not an easy one, I'm sure. Living in the same place for 40 years, then uprooting yourself without all the familiar things you are used to would be tough. We gave her our master bedroom to live in; it was almost the size of a studio minus a kitchen. I wanted her to be comfortable, she continued life for the next fourteen months in our home with her grandchildren. At that time, they ranged from ages five to eleven. Madison was nine at the time and seemed to be the closest to my mom. She would sit with her every night and watch "*Who wants to be a millionaire?*"

My mom had regular monthly doctor's appointments after she came down with pneumonia just a few months into living with us. She was hospitalized for a few days, and after that she was unable to walk on her own. She was wheelchair bound from then on. It is a difficult thing to watch someone you love (even if the relationship was not as one had wished) deteriorate before your eyes. Self inflicted harm to one's body is not something I will ever understand.

SIXTEEN

My mom continued to have several doctors' appointments over the next few months. Her prognosis basically stayed the same, she was very weak but still kept bi-weekly hair appointments, and kept up on her letter and card sending. She never did become familiar enough with a computer, so there were the times she would have me email one of her friends for her if needed.

One day after one of her appointments she wanted to stop at a Christian bookstore we would drive by to look for more notecards. I remember well as a small child the long top drawer of the china cabinet in the dining room filled with cards of every occasion, also remembering a bit too well when my mom would have me help her put stamps on some of the three-hundred plus Christmas cards, and getting mad at me if I put one on crooked. This explains where I get my obsessive need for perfection. As she browsed through the store while I pushed her in the wheelchair, she had me stop for her to reach for and examine the boxed set embellished with dragonflies. She sat the box on her lap to take a closer look, deciding to keep them for purchase. I didn't even know she liked dragonflies.

The following day we were having a discussion about the Pope that went bad. I felt that she was raising him to too high of a level. All I said was," I'm not kissing any man's hand unless it's Jesus himself." She got pretty mad and told me not to dis her Pope.

For the next three days I had Madison bring in my mom's meals for her. Then the next time I absolutely had to go in to her room she said to me; "I love you hon." "I love you too mom."

The next two weeks were normal and all was well; I decided to watch the movie *Dragonfly* one night alone. I felt a very strong notion to sleep on the couch that night putting me much closer to where my mom slept, just in case she needed me. The next morning around six, I was awakened by my mother calling me more loudly than usual in a slurring sounding voice. I literally flew off the couch and ran down the hallway to her room, sliding past the closed double doors before regaining my slipper covered feet. I grabbed and turned both door handles and pushing forward at the same time forcing them wide open. She told me she had knocked her glass of water off from the nightstand and was concerned of the possible mess that it may have left. I told her it was only water and not to worry. She then proceeded to tell me she had to go to the bathroom. I had been assisting her with this for some time now, only this time she was unable to even sit up on her own in the bed. Her slurred speech was getting worse which was very concerning to me, as I scooped her up out of the bed and put her in the wheelchair, she became lethargic while her eyes rolled back in her head. After pushing her just a few feet towards the bathroom she acted as if she was losing conciseness. I began to get very upset and irrational, leaving her in the wheelchair while I proceeded to run all the way down the hall to the kitchen to use that phone to dial 911 when there was a phone right there in her room on the nightstand.

I ran back to her, myself now in tears, telling her the paramedics were on their way. At this point she was breathing erratically and gasping for breath, this of course made me cry even harder despite my trying to be strong given the situation. Then all of a sudden, she seemed to pull out of it as if nothing happened and said "What?" I guess her maternal instincts kicked in for that brief moment when she realized my distress. Before I knew it, the house was full of both firefighters and paramedic personnel. They pulled her from the wheelchair and laid her on the ground, forcing an oxygen mask on her mouth and hooking electrodes all over her; which she wanted nothing to do with, as she kept trying to pull them off and her nightgown back down that had been disheveled by the attending paramedics. She was then loaded up on to a gurney as they took her from me that day, I grabbed her hand as she was wheeled out of the room and into the hallway, her hand slipping out of mine as the gurney moved away from me. That was the last time I saw her, alive anyway, the morning of January 26th, 2003.

She lived her last fourteen months with me and my children. I would not trade those last days for anything despite our differences. I had remembered that the first thing I wanted when I had turned eighteen was to get away from my mom. We never did see eye to eye, and through all the dysfunction that was in our family I can honestly say that I know that my mom loved me, in her own odd way. After she was gone I felt nothing but guilt about our relationship. For ten months I had nightmares about my mom. I would be with her in places I had never seen before, like an old apartment or a dark cave. In both of these most surreal dreams, actually visons, there was a dark presence of some kind that I was trying to get away from, but could not. It was not something I could see, but only feel. In the vision of the cave my mom was there, as she took my hand leading me down the dark and damp jagged stone chiseled-like walkway. I could hear the water trickling down the walls as we moved down the dirt floor. As we rounded the corner turning to the right, we stopped. She then pointed her finger towards the end of the path directing my attention to the black iron barred enclosed jail cell. Instant terror and panic rushed through me from what I saw in the corner of the cell, it was her hanging by her neck. She looked very sick, just as she did right before she died. Frozen in that moment from insurmountable fear, I forced myself awake as I always do in these types of dreams/visions, caught my breath, and slept with a light on for days. I was so depressed over those many months after her death, but then something happened. It was right after Thanksgiving, she had come to me in what, at first, seemed like just a dream. The direct quote from my journal, dated November 29, 2003 reads as follows:

I was with someone in the back of a Catholic church. The service had just ended as I went outside through a side door and walked to a bench to sit. She [my mom] came and sat next to me. She hugged me tight, I did not want to let her go.

Whoever was standing near me could not see her. My mom and I went to a room where she sat in a chair and I on the floor. Everything around us was white. I couldn't see definition of walls or of the floor, or anything. It was just pure whiteness, as was the chair my mom sat in. I asked her questions. "Did you see God?" "Yes." "What does He look like?" "Time." "Is dad there?" She said, "Yes, but he is grumpy." I thought it odd he was there, I hope this is true. I asked if Nick [my brother] was there. She said, "No, he is with the one as old as God." She told me she has a long journey still ahead there, always busy. At that time, I had an overwhelming feeling that my mom understood that what I believe, and what she believed while here on earth, were the same thing. It didn't matter – Christian or Catholic. She saw her mom there, my grandma. And she [mom] was in perfect health, she looked as she did in her thirties. Then there was this buzzing sound and she had to go, "No! wait!" I said as I felt myself being physically sucked back to my room. I actually felt my body hit my bed, like I had fallen from a very high elevation.

That was my first experience with the Other Side. Call it astral travel, or not, but I know I was not here on this earthly plane. Though it would be a few more years before I would begin to experience all that was to come, my interest was certainly piqued after that.

I know now that it was all the guilt, that I felt prior to that experience that caused the nightmares with my mom's strange dark presence. From there leading me to my encounter with her in a place somewhere between here and where she is now; is what gave me the peace I needed to move on, and away from the darkness of guilt, and into the light of nothing but truth.

SEVENTEEN

*T*he summer of 2004 was tryouts for STORM volleyball club which were held at San Bernardino Valley College. The coaches that led these teams were some of the best in the circuit. Mariah made the first string 14's team; the number representing the age group, though she was still thirteen at the time.

It was here that I met the woman who would later become my wife. There was a girl named Tiffani that ended up being picked for the same team as Mariah. Tiffani's dad brought her to the practices in the beginning. He and I had trade conversations with his construction background, and my painting experiences. He seemed nice enough. One night while I was watching the girls' scrimmage on the court, I had an overwhelming feeling to tell Mariah she needed to get to know that girl. Once they had finished a water break, Mariah went back on the court and extended her hand to Tiffani under the net.

They became fast friends and started spending the night at each other's homes. The downfall was the distance between our homes was far more than a skip and a jump.

Over the next few months, I started to get to know Tiffani's mom, Pam, during the drop offs and pickups of our daughters from each other's homes. Naturally at this time I not only had not started to transition, but I also never thought I ever would. I still refused to watch anything on television or a movie that pertained to anything that had to do with transsexual people, knowing that I was one of them. In my mind at the time, I felt I had to continue to dedicate my time to only raising my four kids since I was truly their mother. I was in a marriage of complete disorder in my mind, but I continued to pretend all was well. I put God and church first and tried to raise my kids to do the same.

Even though throughout all the years I stayed in denial while straight women would become attracted to me, I kept pushing my true self back down. Every summer there was club volleyball tournaments in Reno, Nevada. Girls ages 12-18 came from all over North America to compete. It was there that I got to know Pam better. She was in a sixteen year mentally abusive marriage, and I was twelve years in to the biggest mistake of my life for sure. To this day I like to recall the first time I saw Pam at a practice sitting all the way at the top of the bleachers with her head in a textbook. She was tall, even while sitting, and was wearing light faded maroon colored Levis that came up to much above her waist. Her hair was up in what I like to call a whale spout, she argues that description to this day.

When I was able to speak to Mariah during the practice, I whispered to her; "That must be Tiffani's mom."

I was not attracted to her, and she later told me she thought for sure I was a lesbian; a manly one at that. Over that weekend not only did we spend time together, but we seemed to begin to feel maybe something more than a friendship. Pam was totally unfamiliar with what she felt being I was technically a woman. I hate even typing that. After that weekend, I was off to Texas with my family to visit old childhood friends who are sisters, both got married to success minded men and moved there, both the sisters were teachers. After some time, their parents sold their home, the same street I grew up on, and moved themselves to be near there children, and later grandchildren.

On that trip I wanted to kill Patrick, I had just totally had it with him, and his passive aggressive nature. When we returned home there was a message from Pam telling me she had bought two Journey tickets and asked if I wanted to go even though Journey is not the same without Steve Perry. I must say the stand in that year was pretty damn good with your eyes closed. On our way to the concert, we stopped and ate at an Applebee's.

By now, I had to tell her about my past, and that I had started to transition twenty years prior, and the reason I stopped at that time. She was a bit floored by my story, but then began to understand how she became attracted to me. Her first question after my story was if I would transition now. I immediately said no. I told her I just couldn't do that to my kids.

Over the next several weeks we talked more and more on the phone, I even asked for her advice about "the blond one" I hadn't seen her or even spoke to her for quite some time. She wanted to meet up with me to talk, so I thought I would get Pam's opinion. There was a time when I would have wanted things to somehow workout between me and the blonde one, and even though I did decide to go see her the only thing I was thinking about was Pam. When I was on my way home from the encounter the traffic going north on interstate 15 was horrible as usual, so I called Pam and asked her if I could stop by her place to wait out the slow drive up the hill through the pass. She said she was alone, and said it was fine that I dropped in. The feelings that we shared, but didn't speak of, were that of a typical crush. It was very obvious to both of us that the attraction was undeniable.

Every day after that we not only continued to call each other, there were also the daily emails, later deemed *the email chronicles.* It was obvious what was happening, so we took it to another level. We planned out a trip to Montana with the vision of looking at properties with the ridiculous possibility of us moving both families, even the husbands at the time. What was becoming more difficult for me, was my true physical identity yet again. On November 5th, 2005, we left for our six-day trip, knowing that we would be spending the night at hotels along the way, I couldn't even begin to fathom how anything physical between us was going to actually happen. Our first stop was Las Vegas, and the moment we hit the room we were all over each other, imagine that. We were in the dark, only removing shirts, while making out over an extended amount of time. That was as far as things went that night.

The next night we found ourselves in Idaho Falls, the man behind the desk referred to me as Ben Reed, Pam's married name at the time was Reed. We never quite figured that one out. What we did know for sure was the sexual tension between us was becoming even more elevated. We went down to the bar to have a couple of drinks, which is something I very rarely do, but didn't want her to think I never drank, even though I didn't. Upon returning to the room, it was just as it was the night before but this time all clothes came off. Pure darkness was certainly required by me. This would be the first time I would ever lay with a woman without an artificial penis close at hand. As great as it felt between the two of us, I knew I couldn't continue on in that way, my mind now screaming *I am not a woman!*

Not only did I require a dick to have sex with a woman, I was still continuously fighting against my true self, along with the guilt I was feeling about what my decision could do to my kids. I tried in some small way to end what was started with Pam, to spare them the pain and the fallout of my transition. Pam, on the other hand told me she loved me as I was, even though she had never in her life been attracted to a woman. She would have settled as being labeled a lesbian by her family and the world. That was a complete impossibility for me. I simply told her that I cannot continue in a relationship, with her, as a female. I never felt or identified as a lesbian and wasn't going to start now, its just not that simple. Even as early as it was into this very strange and new way Pam felt about a person born female, she was more than fine with it. I on the other hand was not. I couldn't understand that she didn't understand why I absolutely needed to transition and become a man on a physical level.

I came to learn how incredibly complex and broad the sliding scale of gender identity really was, and came to know that I was much more of a minority than I ever would have thought. In my mind along with most other people's thoughts there are two genders, male and female, this is true most of the time, but not always. There have been male babies born with one ovary and one testicle, just as noted female babies have been born with a penis of sorts and an opening for a vagina. This is not as rare as you might think, and happens more often then is talked about. The new parents are then left with the decision to chose which gender their new baby is to be. Can you even imagine making that choice? What if you make the wrong choice? Meaning the choice made ends up not matching the child's brain as time goes on. These cases are called Ambiguous Biological Identities.

This was not my case, though there were times I had wished it were, thinking it would have given me more proof than just my oversized clitoris as to why I innately felt male my entire life. The truth is I had a lot to learn about what is called the identity spectrum. It's not enough to be trapped in a physical body that your mind is opposite from, which was my case, so naturally I figured all those who were born like myself were exactly the same. For instance, being born female and attracted to females, only through a male brain is very different than simply being gay and attracted to the same sex. But wait, there is more confusion I was not aware of. There are born females that transition to males, that are attracted to males. What? I really didn't understand that at all for a very long time.

See, I never identified as part of the LGBT and now Q community. Also, I never thought the "T" needed to be there, thinking that all transsexual people that transition to the opposite sex they were born, were naturally only attracted to what is now opposite of themselves. Am I making sense? I am the one that looks at gender and sexual orientation as being black and white.

EIGHTEEN

Thanksgiving that year was meant to be shared between our two families, but prior to that day Patrick's father died in North Carolina, so he grabbed the first flight out. Also, the week we returned from Montana, Pam had asked Eric for a divorce, although she was still in their home. Pam then decided to bring Tiffani with her and come spend Thanksgiving weekend with me and my kids. Pam had never been in an extramarital affair, and she was very conflicted with the dishonesty she had been living. Upon Pam's arrival back to her home she came clean to Eric about her relationship with me. Naturally all hell broke loose!

He called everyone they knew and reported that Pam was now a lesbian. After 3 weeks of pure hell Pam left Eric on December 19th 2005. She stayed with us in my house, and yes Patrick was there. He knew what was going on and realized he didn't have any control over me. On February 18th, 2006, Pam moved into a one-bedroom apartment in Rancho Cucamonga, since she worked in neighboring Ontario. Making the drive from Apple Valley was becoming a bit too grueling as well.

At the time I was a security guard for a collection of stores spanning two blocks in Rancho Cucamonga, patrolling on a bicycle riding between those businesses collecting check-in signatures from each store, proving that I was there doing my job. I now could stay at Pam's apartment if I didn't want to make that drive home myself. In March 2006 I made the decision that I absolutely could not continue on any longer as a woman despite the fact I had four children. I made the call to the Los Angeles Gender Center in March and spoke to Amanda Silvestri, a counselor/gender specialist. During our phone conversation due to the fact that my voice was already deeper than a typical female, she was under the impression that I wanted to transition from male to female! Once we got that all straightened out my first appointment was set for April 8th, 2006.

In the meantime, I had to break this news to my kids that I was going to transform from a woman to a man. At the end of March Pam and I took Mariah and Tiffani to see Ellen DeGeneres, at NBC studios in Burbank. Eric had no idea Pam was taking her there, and sure enough we were on camera that day in the audience and had feared someone might have seen us and tell Eric. With all the waiting you must do prior to getting into the studio, I decided I would break this news to Mariah first. First born, first one to know, I guess. She took it pretty hard. Her first and really only question was why I could not wait until they were older before doing such a thing. Mariah and I had a very close bond right from her birth, though on that day it was broken. From then on and even now, she mourns the death of her mother. Our relationship will never be the same. I too miss the way things used to be between the two of us.

Madison and Jennifer seemed to take it better than Mariah, accepting if for what it was, I don't really know why, or even how true that may be, at least with Madison, who has a tendency to hide her true feelings to remain neutral. My son, Jonathan, was only nine at the time and didn't have much of a reaction that I can remember. Though at eighteen, he would randomly ask questions that were not always easy to answer. I had told him that I never should have had any kids, at least not it the way I did, giving birth myself. Not once, but four times only trying to be something I just wasn't. Hoping that somehow it would whip me into the woman I was physically. Clearly that did not work, it only left emotional scars on me. Jonathan viewed my explanation as if I didn't love them. I said to him, "How can you love children that never existed?" That is the only way I can process that regret.

I began to spend more nights with Pam in her apartment, as I knew I could not transition in front of my kids. On April 17th 2006

I was with Pam at her place, we were naked in bed. All of a sudden there was loud pounding, first on the front door as if it might collapse inward, then moments later on the bedroom window making us jump out of bed sending Pam running to hide in the closet out of sheer panic knowing now it was Eric yelling at us outside the window. Apparently, he had been casing the joint and waited until he spotted my truck there to make his raging move. Pam ended up having a complete and total meltdown in that closet, I was unable to physically contain her while she spun out of control mentally. She didn't want me to confront him for the real fear he might kill me, which kept me from opening the door.

There was no consoling her, I took her back up to my house over that weekend; I was not going to leave her alone now with Eric on yet another tirade. On Monday she admitted herself to Kaiser for having suicidal thoughts, which in turn posted guard at her door and sent for an ambulance to take her to the Loma Linda psych ward, she was there for nine days in a locked unit. I visited her every day. Eric tried to get in to see her, he was not allowed. His mother brought Tiffani in to see her. The day before her birthday Pam was released and I moved in permanently with her.

In June of 2006 with my hormone letter in hand I had received from Amanda, I went to my first appointment with Dr. Richard Horowitz in Los Angeles to begin taking testosterone. After that first shot in the office, Pam has administered them ever since, every two weeks. What would have I done without her, really? On August 7th, 2006, my top surgery was performed by Dr. Michael Brownstein in San Francisco. That day, was the first day I began to feel free since puberty. What was removed from my body is what had defined what I was on the outside for so many years. Despite being mistaken on the phone as a man when I was not trying to be one, and even when my chest was bound as tight as possible and getting away with passing as a young man twenty years before, they were still there heinously hanging off me at the end of the day, reflecting back in every bathroom mirror I stood before.

That day I was overcome with relief, upon feeling my chest through the tightly wrapped bandages; the absence of that physical burden that was there no more. The recovery process of a double mastectomy and a little master sculpting, is a painful one. Constant pain medication is required over the first few days along with having to dump the drainage tubes that hung from my sides. My memories from leaving the surgery center are spotty at best. I am one that has a terrible time coming out from sedation, then feel like what I assume is complete drunkenness, since I have never been in that condition. The medical staff informed Pam she needed to pay for parking before loading me up. The parking structure was set up so you take a parking ticket upon entry, then to be able to exit, you pay the attendant that was on the fifth floor; you then receive a new ticket to insert into the machine at the exit enabling the mechanical arm to lift allowing a vehicle's passage. The back door of the facility where I would be waiting for Pam was on the third floor of the parking structure. It took some time just getting me into the car with Pam having to stabilize me on my feet, then guide me in and on to the seat along with the task of buckling me in. By the time we made it down to the exit and inserted the ticket, the arm didn't raise, followed by a digital message displayed on the screen that read, Time limit exceeded, add additional funds. By now, a rather long line of cars was forming behind us. I was still extremely drowsy from sedation, going in and of consciousness.

The attendant had the ability to speak through the machine and said we were going to have to go back to the fifth floor and pay the additional money. Even if Pam agreed that the additional money was warranted, what the parking attendant was asking was completely impossible. With the unending cars behind us, the only possible way to move was forward which would be crashing through the gate. I was jolted awake by Pam screaming at the attendant to let us out as we had already paid and it was beyond her control how long it took to load me up and get down to this exit! Next, the guy from the car behind us decided to walk up to our car to see what the hell was going on, causing Pam to scream at him as well. In my semi-drugged state, I said "Go get 'em baby". Pam had completely lost her mind, but eventually the attendant came down from his little enclosure to push the red panic button on the wall to open the gate for us.

When we arrived back to the place we were staying, I was still in pretty bad shape. The place was designed for privacy offering individual cabin type units. Pam came around to my side of the car pulling me up and out, on to my feet the best she could, then guided me to and up the three concrete steps to the vibrant red door. Once we were in, she put me to bed keeping an eye on me and draining the fluid from the bulbs that hung from the sides of my new chest. The next morning still in and out of consciousness I listened to Pam's words the best I could. She had reminded me that she had to leave and fly back to Ontario that very day for a court hearing concerning the custody of her children. My half sister Stephanie, who lived in the Bay area would come to sit with me until Pam's return later that evening. Have I mentioned yet of Pam's incredible devotion to me?

After Pam kissed my head. and bid me good-bye, assuring me that Stephanie was on her way, my cell phone rang that sat on the nightstand next to the bed. Answering it in my weak and groggy state I said "Hello?" "Please come and get me away from him!" Mariah had said through sobbing tears, making reference to Patrick. "Honey, I'm not even there, I just had surgery here in San Francisco." "Please! I can't stay here another day!" The rest of the call is a blur as I faded out of reality again. She ended up calling Susan, whom she felt was the next best thing to a family member. She did not hesitate to instruct Mariah to pack her things while promising she would be right over to get her. As much as I was relieved that Mariah was able to escape the moment in which she found herself trapped and distressed, her mind viewed me as abandoning her in my absence that day. I know deep down, that she knew there was nothing I would not do for her, but her pain of losing her mother she so desperately needed made her heart grow cold towards me.

Our relationship would never be the same, and it broke my own heart that day. Six years later, on her twenty-second birthday, she asked us if she could have a few friends over, seven maybe eight, we told her sure as we went off to the third level of our townhome to our bedroom. The small gathering wasn't set to start just yet, and we were tired. A few hours later, we were awakened to the echoing sounds of laughing over the din of the many conversations that were bouncing off the concrete walls of the three-story buildings that lined both sides of the blacktop alley-way down below. I pulled myself up out of bed thinking some rude neighbor was having a big party into what was approaching a new day.

When I reach the second floor, which was the main living floor, the conversations and laughing had now filled my head and for good reason. When I approached the open dinning/kitchen area I couldn't believe my eyes! Past the dining space, through the wide- open French doors leading to the balcony, there wasn't just seven or eight friends, but thirty! Some standing, some sitting, and even some hanging over the balcony. I went over and scanned the crowd until I spotted Mariah then waved her to come over into the house. "What is happening? This is not seven or eight! It's after midnight and they all have to go now!" She turned away from me and went back out to the balcony to inform the crowd that the party was over. Quickly, the herd of shuffling feet began to file in to the room, down the steps, and out of the house. Before I even had a chance to make my way back up the steps to get back to bed, Mariah came at me in a highly escalated rant right up close, and in my face and said, "Do you know how much you have fucked-up my life!?" This made me realize how drunk she was, then she went to grab me as I pushed her away while she continued to scream at me, I couldn't understand why this was happening as her words faded in my ears trying to block the pain of what was now happening, and what was to be. She moved out of the house and away from me the very next day. Sheer guilt is all I could feel, nothing more, no love left to be found from my own child in that moment.

The glimpse of sun-light I saw through the sheer linen blind that hung in the window, seemed to quickly turn into night. I hardly remember Stephanie sitting in the chair that sat in the corner while she read a book, while the next thing I remembered was Pam at my side rousing me awake enough to drain the bulbs of fluid that would remain for eight more days, until I returned for my follow-up visit with Dr. Brownstein. During those days we stayed in the room as I began to recover, Pam had to help me with everything from getting dressed to getting into the shower. The pain was pretty intense if I even attempted to raise my arms above my waist. With the arrival of the eighth and final day of my confinement, we were both ready to get back home, but first the drainage bulbs needed to be removed, then receive a clean bill of health. Dr. Brownstein was among some of the very best top surgery doctors in the nation, leading to stellar results of many, now myself included. This was certainly the reason I chose him as my surgeon after viewing many impressive photos of his work. The outcome of such a surgery had a lot to do with one's body mass before hand. If someone is overweight their outcome will not be the same as someone that is not. Removing breasts is the easy part for a surgeon, it's the sculpting of the pecs that is most important when becoming a man, and Dr. Brownstein was a master. Yes, there are scar lines, but very faint and become hidden from chest hair if you have enough, but normally will go unnoticed unless someone is doing a very close inspection of your new chest.

NINETEEN

ABSOLUTELY LIFE CHANGING!

After six weeks of healing, the first thing I was gong to do was to go shirtless! This was a dream to say the least. First, I would walk around Pam's apartment without a shirt, then walk into the bathroom to view the reality of what only used to be in my mind was pure bliss! It took me some time before I ventured outside without a shirt, but not because of how it looked (which was, and still is fabulous) but mentally afraid somehow someone would know, of course they never did, it just took time to get past all that. I was beginning to feel much more comfortable in public and needed to find a job after being off for the last few months.

I walked into the Bed Bath & Beyond in Riverside and had run right into a very short woman, whom I assumed was just an hourly employee since she was pulling around a cage filled with merchandise putting items in their proper places in the front of the store. It turned out she was the store manager, and her name was Lynn. I asked if she was hiring, she said yes and went to get me an application to take and fill out, which I did in the car while sitting in the parking lot. I brought it back in and handed it back to Lynn. After we were home for a couple of hours, she called me and asked if I wanted to come in the following day for an interview, I of course accepted. I arrived early to the store the next day, I am always punctual. She saw me walk in and said, "Marco, follow me and we can get started." I fell in line right behind her to a door in the hallway that led up to the office. Her desk sat next to the wall facing out towards the floor, to have a birds' eye view through the smoked glass window that spanned the upper part of the wall. A good security tactic for spotting shop lifters while someone is up there at that desk anyway.

The interview went rather quick and very well, even though I was nervous still feeling like people may somehow know I was born female. I could actually feel the sweat running down my chest as my heart beat faster from the thought. She hired me on the spot, and I started working there on October 31st.

After a few months, I began feeling tingling in my hands, and figured it was a circulation thing while I would clap my hands together trying to get it to stop. My job title was Freight Flow Lead and I replaced a person that had left the job and never came back. This made me be one of the first people in the store very early, long before it opened.

For those of you familiar with the layout of these particular stores, you will know how merchandise hangs on pegs that are fitted into hidden slotted strips that span across white corrugated pressboard. The reason I bring this up is because it can be quite a physical task to pull one of the pegs out, they cannot just come loose and fall off on their own.

Then came the morning when it all started to happen. I came in at 5am as usual along with the opening manger and one other employee, to help me pull out the freight from the stockroom on U-boats and metal cages with shelves. Just like every other morning before this one, I was walking the wooden floor towards the back of the store to the stockroom. Halfway down, scattered all over the floor in my path was eight digital cameras still hooked on the pegs by the hole in the plastic at the top. No one had been in the store since the night before when the doors were closed and locked as everyone left for their homes. There is absolutely no way an employee could have gotten away with such nonsense since the closing manager walks the store before they all are allowed to leave together. *Someone or something* pulled out every peg and threw them on the pathway on that side on the store. At that moment

I knew that something else was there in that store other than people. It was then that I started to understand that what I was feeling in my hands was energy: *their* energy. I went to Lynn and asked her if I could set up a video recorder and let it run over night. Surprisingly she said yes.

The following evening, I drove back over there 30 minutes before the store closed to pick a spot to set up the camera. I used a Handy cam Vision video Hi8, which is now obsolete, and has become a collector's item. My how fast things change. I placed it across three metal pegs aimed towards the room where all the picture frames and artwork resided. It contained a two hour reel to reel tape. I purposely filmed on a Friday night so I would be able to view it immediately the next day since I was off on weekends. When I woke up on Saturday morning I flew out of bed, and down to the store before it opened, trying to be patient while tapping on the glass door waiting for someone to notice me and let me in. Finally, after what seemed like forever, a co-worker strolled over towards the door unlatching the lock. "Hey Mar…" is all she got out before I blew past her saying, I'm just here to grab my camera and get it back home to review the film!"

I sat down at my kitchen table, rewound the film and hit play. I stared with anticipation for what seemed like an eternity. If it hadn't been for the overhead music that was left on over night, I certainly would have fallen asleep at the table. With only twelve minutes of footage left I had pretty much lost all hope while waiting for the tape to get to the end and the screen to turn blue. Then, something happened…. the camera started to move back and forth as if someone was slowly panning. I could not believe what I was seeing, and nearly fell out of my chair with excitement! The other part of the recording that proved interesting was the kind of audio that was picked up. The pegs on which the camera sat are in the candle room. Inside that room, are those mesh bags filled with glass beads used for aquariums and other art projects. Many times in the two hour span there was the sound of one of those glass pieces being thrown or simply dropped. Another sound picked up on the second tape was a loud crash that came from the other side of the store. This made me think I should start recording audio over there as well. I didn't own an audio recorder at the time so I ended up bringing in one of those handheld units that used the small micro tapes. Pam had it from when she was trying to record Eric in one of his tirades.

One night when the store was about to close, I took the recorder to the stock room and turned it on. I waited a few minutes while I asked a question or two. After I shut it off I returned to the front of the store where all the closing employees were assembled. I sat in one of the summer lounge chairs on display. I rewound the tape and hit the playback button. I could not believe what I was hearing! It sounded horrifying! I gathered everyone around so they too could hear the creepy ass voice attempting to communicate. The closing manager of the night, Lara said, "That does not sound good." She told Pam not to listen to it before bed. She listened to it on our way home and said it sounded like Pinhead from Hell Raiser! When we got home, I decided to keep listening and heard the closing of the store announcement which was done by Lara, but it was very slow just like Pinhead's. It turned out that I was Pinhead since the slow play switch on the side of the recorder had been on! I was so mad and Pam was laughing so hard. I told her not to tell Lara! I felt so stupid thinking some evil spirit was lurking in the store! I knew that I had to take a step forward and invest in a real digital recorder.

Over the next eight and a half months I recorded every single day at both home and work. Yes, with a real digital recorder with a USB port in order to transfer the audio files into the computer to be analyzed in a program much like one used in recording music. When an EVP (electronic voice phenomena) is found within a file I highlighted it and saved it. EVP's have different classifications of "A ,B, or C" a class" A" sounds like people speaking as we do, a "B" file is some people can understand what was said, but not all people. "C" I didn't even bother to save since they are inaudible. Class "A" was all I would ever present for others to hear. From my daily devotion of journaling, my recorded conversations with what I call key spirits, a book was born called _Paranormal Noise: Listen Beyond the Silence._ It is both educational and entertaining, I have even recorded death.

I had been told by an established author while the manuscript was being put together that only four percent of new authors are published a year worldwide, that was thirteen years ago, I had sent the story out to a few publishers to no avail. My only choice was to self- publish it. It was not a cheap process to say the least, and now have learned it totally depends on who you publish with, if you must do it on your own. However, at the time it was something I had to do. I had learned too much, and now knew too much about the Other Side to not share it with other people. Believe me, death is not black and white.

However, without a literary agent, or any other media support, thirteen years later book sales certainly have not soared through the roof!

It's funny how long ago I actually started this book, long before it was ready to be written, back when we still used typewriters. I don't want to write it for nothing, to end up in a box with other "important" papers only to be found by one of my children after my death. Now is the time, now I'm ready to share it, knowing it will shock those to their core who has only known me as Marco. That is what one wants after transitioning, but all not able to experience such joy if they fail to not "pass" as the gender they have transitioned into. This seems to happen to more male to female, than does for female to male people, and with good reason. Since most biological men are taller and normally have more muscle mass, it's not as easy for them to transition as smoothly as many female to male people can and have, though there are always exceptions. Short biological men do exist, as do very tall biological females, often leaving society puzzled at times by those with whom they cross paths. I can be just as puzzled by those I encounter, finding myself taking note of secondary characteristics about someone I am unsure of, such as the size of their hands, the way they walk, and sound of their voice. Many times, male to female people will still sound male despite their efforts of dressing female. Even if they happen to be taking female hormones and testosterone blockers, a male to female has to *train* their voice to be higher. Though again, not that there are not biological women with lower voices. Sadly, many male to female people end up looking like a drag queen, not being taken seriously.

It is much more easier for a female to transition into a male. Testosterone lowers the voice, and in my case, mine was already lower than most. Now, some of these people end up sounding a little like a chipmunk, which is never good. My point is, if after transitioning and the person is unable to blend right into society, it can be mentally devastating. Blending into society means both your gender and sex identity are in sync as you walk past anyone and realize they have no reason to doubt you are the gender in which you have now become. No more worries about people doing a double take, or looking back at you as you've passed wondering… *Was that a man, or a woman?*

TWENTY

After my top surgery had been completed, I set my sights on bottom surgery. I had been doing a lot of research on the two options available and looking at pictures of results from the doctors I was considering contacting to get more information and pricing. Money was always an issue, hence the reason I sold my Cadillac Escalade for cash to pay for my top surgery. I had it nailed down to two surgeons; Toby Meltzer in Arizona, and Gary Alter in Beverly Hills, California. They both had impressive photos of their work, and pricing was similar; but driving to Los Angeles was much more appealing than Arizona. I received an email from Dr. Alter's personal secretary, Zena, asking me if I would be interested in meeting with him to talk about being on the Dr. 90210 television show as his subject for what would be his only episode that season. My initial response to myself was no way. However, if I were to agree to appear on this episode called *Transparent* my cost for the surgery would be drastically cut.

The thought of being on national television and then people knowing what I really was struck me as horrifying. I waited for Pam to get home to discuss it with her. After I read the email a second time, the line that stuck out was that I would be helping people like me by sharing my story. I emailed her back and agreed to meet with Dr. Alter to discuss it further. There is something about Beverly Hills that cannot be denied, Rodeo Drive just makes you feel as wealthy as those you pass on the sidewalks, as Dr. Alter's office is right around the corner of the famed street. The pleasure was both of ours upon meeting each other.

He loved the way I looked, and I was pretty taken by his personality right from the start. He mentioned he had already interviewed another guy from Texas to possibly shoot the segment with but told me I have the spot if I wanted it.

We sat and discussed how the surgery is performed and looked at, and held, silicone testicles he had there in his office. It was all a part of deciding on which size to go with. I was opting for the larger ones myself, but he talked me into the smaller stating that it's best for the end result to penis size ratio. I still wish I had insisted on the bigger ones.

The surgery I opted for is called a metoidioplasty. Generally, the enlarged clitoris, which is an effect of testosterone hormone replacement therapy (HRT), is relocated upwards to create a sensate and functioning micro-penis. The surrounding skin of the clitoris is removed and "released" from the pubis to give the impression of more length. This results in a circumcised appearance, although patients may opt for an uncircumcised look. The suspensory ligament may be partially divided. Labial ligaments and the urethral plate are released, which allows the penis to extend further outward. The procedure also involves the creation of a glans and scrotum by using the tissue from the labia majora or labia minora with two testicle prosthetics.

Now, with all the medical tech talk behind us, I chose that route for a very good reason. The penis is far from that of a biological man, but all the sensitivity is there in the same way as a natural penis, versus the other option which is called a phalloplasty, where by skin grafting from your body a penis is built. Yes, the size is much greater, but in order to maintain an erection, an erectile prosthetic device needs to be installed whereas with the metoidioplasty the erection happens on it's own.

Filming began the first week of March 2008 at our apartment in Riverside, California. It was a big week for us since we were scheduled to be married on the 8th. Naturally the producer felt it would be great to film in Las Vegas and include our wedding footage in the episode, making our wedding nationally televised. It was a fun experience walking outside the hotel with a camera crew in tow, people wondering who in the hell is this guy and his woman? I would like to say all went well, and it did for the producer, but certainly not for us as far as happy ceremony expectations. The most important part of the ceremony for both Pam and I was the music. Her entrance was supposed to be Pachelbel's Cannon in D. Instead, they threw on the cliché Wedding March "Here comes the Bride" how incredibly boring is that? And if that wasn't bad enough, not only was the wedding chapel crew not able to make the CD play that we brought for us to go back down the aisle, instead there was nothing. Yes, I said nothing...complete silence. We both were crushed over that, and still are to this day fourteen years later.

My song choice was "Love Comes Walking In" by Van Halen. E! Entertainment said there would be copyright issues. Then we decided to go with "Breathless" by "The Corrs." One day in my mind I want us to do it over with the music on both sides of the ceremony. I figure we just were not worth the hassle to get the permission from Van Halen. It's now a bucket list item.

Due to my work schedule the events were not filmed in chronological order. My bottom surgery was done on March 13th, 2008, five days later. My reduced cost was the exact amount of my tax return that year, right down to the dollar. Strangely enough the physical recovery of a bottom surgery is not as painfully bad as top surgery. If it were not for Pam being by my side the entire time through both of them, life would have been a bit too physically challenging during those times. God, I love her.

Before my bottom surgery, I used a pants stuffer; a fake limp penis to fill my pants with a bulge. It's an absolute must for many transmen, and for me I figured I still would need one to feel secure walking around in public. One thing I did know for a fact; is that many more women than will admit, drop their eyes down to a guy's package area. I've had it happen enough times for me to notice. I tried to continue this practice out of total insecurity, but realized it actually started to get in the way of what was now my own penis. Let me elaborate a bit on a transman's penis; the ones that opt for a metoidioplasty. Just like biological males, there are all different sizes. No, not to the extreme size as a bio male, but we have to take what we can get. I was fortunate enough to have been born with an oversized clitoris, and once testosterone is present long enough, the now micro- penis will continue to grow. No, not at an alarming rate, (I wish) but certainly for some of us it can be pretty substantial given what we've got to work with. Depending on the actual length of the micro-penis will determine if penetration is possible. Let me say that I'm good in that area. Never satisfied with it, oddly like many bio-men, but I'm able to do it; some people never will experience that with their own.

Prior to the airing of my episode "*Transparent*" I had the pleasure of being on the *Tim Conway Jr* radio show in Los Angeles along with Pam, and Dr. Alter to promote the episode. The first thing I said to Tim before we were going on the air was, "I love your dad". Which in turn prompted him to tell us the story of the day of his own birth, that while his dad (Tim senior) was working on the set of the show *McHale's Navy*, that aired from 1962 through 1966, he received the call that his wife was in labor and rushed right to the hospital wearing his Navy uniform from the show. Everyone who saw him thought he was actually serving in the Navy. During a commercial break Tim said to me, "We should go to a Dodger's game together sometime." As great as that would have been, my mind began thinking of how a friendship with this man could lead me to the infiltration into Carol Burnett's house! Neither happened, I am sad to report.

CLASS REUNION OF 1983

We made a plan to stay with Kenzie and her family in Indiana for a week in October of 2008. During that week Kenzie, Pam and I would take a short road trip to Ottawa to attend our 25-year reunion. Both excited and nervous, Pam and I flew into Indianapolis and Kenzie picked us up at the airport. Pam nervous because she had only met Kenzie briefly at our wedding earlier that year and this was the first opportunity for them to get to know each other. I was nervous because I was presenting as a man twenty-five years later. The only people present that knew of my new identity were Laurie Hicks and Kenzie. All others had to be introduced to me since I was completely unrecognizable. The woman that approached our table was now married to the same James that wanted to marry me at fifteen. Laurie asked her, "Do you know who this is?" pointing to me. With no immediate answer, Laurie revealed my birth name. The woman then responded by saying, "Oh yeah, you look thinner." We all looked at each other perplexed by such a response. Clearly, she went and told James *who* she had encountered, so when we ran into them later in the evening, I offered my hand for a handshake. With no eye contact and head down, he quickly shook my hand while choking out, "hey man". Pam found this hilarious! The good news is that the majority of people not only accepted me as male, but they were also not even surprised remembering how I was back in our school days together.

Another guy, Dan, that was now covered in tattoos, looking like a member of a rock band had said to me, "I must say, you make a fine-looking dude, and I thought I was going to be the surprise of the reunion!" Word got around pretty quick that I was there as the opposite gender than I was born. I had many people approach me telling me how great I looked, women saying that they would pick me up in a bar, all around making me feel just as welcome as if I hadn't changed a bit. The Dr. 90210 episode was set to air just a few days after the reunion, so that was a big topic of conversation.

Pam and I would return to Ottawa 5 years later to attend the 30-year reunion. This time we flew into Chicago and made the 80-mile drive to Ottawa to stay in a remote bed & breakfast. At the ice breaker event the night before the reunion, we were at a bar with a dance floor. Pam was cutting a rug with Kenzie's husband on the dance floor while I was standing alone taking in the music and murmur of the room draped in low lighting. At that moment a very familiar face appeared in front of me and simply said, "There you are, I have been wondering about you for the last thirty years." It was Margot, who was only there because her husband was in my class, but I never knew him. What she said meant everything to me that night. She got it, she understood that all those years ago, the boy within me was always there, but now she could *see* him. We sat and talked the rest of the night, and the next morning Pam and I had breakfast with her and her husband before heading back to California. We remain friends to this day.

Transparent aired in October 2008, and with reality TV shows also came fan pages where viewers would converge and comment about the episodes. When I became aware of this practice, naturally I began reading what was said about the portrayal of my story. Unbelievable ignorance arose in the thread I came across, as someone had blatantly shared their false idea that Pam must be trans too, in this case meaning she was born male, and had transitioned to female. This is the kind of ignorance that really pisses me off. Pam is a biological female. Many biological females date and marry trans-guys, I am not the only one! With just this one example alone goes to show how incredibly ignorant a vast majority of the population really is. Not that I don't understand why someone would think such a thing, since it does happen. As I have mentioned, I personally think the "T" in LGBTQ should not be there, but that is my personal opinion. Many trans people are very much a part of that community, making me more of a minority. There are many trans people that date all kinds of labels that belong to this group, but I was never one to begin with. Gender fluidity is ridiculous to me at this time in our history, these kinds of people have always existed, they just didn't make such a big deal about it.

For those that decide one day to be male, and the next day female, and continue on in this flip flop fashion is very confusing to me. As someone who has struggled with Gender Dysphoria for a lifetime, I feel the direction the Trans community is headed makes a mockery of those that are like me. To me, that makes no sense, unless perhaps you are an actor. Non-binary is a newer term for someone that does not identify male or female, throwing me into an absolute loss of understanding, since now, one of my own children identifies as such. We are not allowed to use he, or she, but rather "they and them." Try that in a sentence or two while maintaining proper sentence structure.

I am all about free expression, I just don't understand the need for so many labels. There are different versions and outcomes to any diversion from being born male or female, with some changing a little, while others their entire appearance. Even if I would have pondered on dating within the trans community, then finding someone that was born male, but now was female, all of them don't have their penis removed, just as all trans- men don't have bottom surgery to now have a penis. These are things I don't understand, and had no reason to put myself through those mental games.

TWENTY-ONE

After working at Bed Bath & Beyond for four years, I was forced out. Lynn had been sent to another store leaving Greg the asshole in charge. He never liked me and tried to get me written up once while Lynn was still there. That didn't happen, she wasn't buying his crap, and told him to let it go. During inventory in 2010 he came up with this bullshit to sabotage me, even having the assistant manager at the time back him up, even though she knew it was a lie. She has apologized for that awhile back now. He brought me into what had become his office, sat me down and told me if I didn't sign the write up, I knew where the door was. I really wanted to punch him, instead, I told him he was full of shit, and I walked out. The only hard part about it was leaving all those active spirits behind. you might ask, "well can't they just follow you?" Oh yes, and a couple of them did.

It took me two solid months of looking every day to find another job. That turned out to be at Home Depot where I ended up meeting Scott, who worked in plumbing. I was in the paint department. After I was there a couple of months, as he was walking by the paint counter one day he stopped, looked at me and said, "I have a question for you, and need to know if it is true." My mind went right to maybe he thinks he knows me from TV and he's on to me, he knows my secret. "Well, that all depends on what the question is." I had said to him. "I heard you wrote a book." "Oh yes, that, yes I did." "My house is haunted for sure, maybe you could come by and check in out?" he said. "No man, I'm not looking to become an investigator." "Just give it some thought,

I can promise you wont be disappointed." This request from Scott was his only reason for his visit to my work area that day, though months later, I would come to know that Scott's wife, Jenny had seen me on Dr. 90210 a few years back, and had recognized me but Scott had never even brought that up upon our first conversation. It simply didn't matter to him. He didn't view me as some kind of oddity, just another guy. When the topic had come up many months later out on his front porch one afternoon, he said it was no big deal since his sister had trans friends when he was growing up. Meaning he was exposed to them, I guess? Again, the spectrum is very broad as I'm sure he was well aware of. However, on another note what was thought to be a glitch in the social security system by the HR woman in our store was another thing.

When I answered the internal call at the paint desk, it was Amani from her office upstairs. "Marco, can you come up and see me for a moment?" She asked. "Sure, I'll be right up." I immediately made my way to the back of the store and up the steep climb of steps to her office door. Walking in, I found her staring at the computer screen as I sat down in the chair in front of her desk. "Hey Marco, the social security office has another name with the same number as yours, I imagine you will have to have that somehow removed." At this point I was utterly horrified, believing I had to tell her I said, "It's not a mistake, that was my birth name, I had a sex change a few years ago." Her face went pale, as she nearly fell out of her chair while clumsily reaching for her walkie-talkie clipped to the waistband of her jeans. She called for her boss, who ran the store, to come up to her office, now I was sweating profusely while we waited for him. Why did she even call him up there? Why did he have to know? Not that I wouldn't have expected her to tell him, who wouldn't? He comes in, says hello, then asks her what was so urgent. She told him what I had said to her, his response was, "And?" Probably knowing she was in the wrong for even sharing such information to another in my presence? I don't even know, but after that happened, word spread like wildfire. An employee took it upon himself to pull up my episode of Dr. 90210 to show as many coworkers as possible in the store that I was indeed transgendered, yet no one ever said a word to me.

Another most interesting day prior to the above incident, was while I and two other guys in paint were having a lull in customers, all three of us noticed and watched a woman...? or...man, walking in our direction. They wore a fitted red sweater with small noticeable breasts underneath, along with tighter blue jeans and brown heeled shoes to match the purse, that was strapped to their arm. *She* was wearing a wig for sure because I knew who *she* was. The closer they got to us, the more apparent it was to the other guys that this person was certainly a man. It was sad, because he was trying so hard, but could not pass as a woman by any means. His name was Dean, and he worked in the produce department where we did our grocery shopping. He was very attentive to his work, and very helpful in the department. He was tall and thin, and normally wore a green apron over his uniform. He was also a back-up cashier when needed. We saw him on a weekly basis and were quite surprised many weeks later when approaching his line with our items. Not only was he not wearing an apron, but a camisole under his white shirt to give coverage to his now developing breasts, from hormone therapy. I for one, would never have been able to transition on the job. That seems like a mental nightmare. Watching my co-workers slightly ridicule Dean, was the day I coined the phrase, *you never know who, or what stands right beside you.*

Nearing the end of 2010, I did go to Scott's house bringing only my digital recorder to do what I did best, record spirits talking. By spending a couple of hours inside what really did turn out to be haunted in every sense off the word, I not only recorded "Art" who is a resident spirit that stays in the black hearse that was his, before Scott owned it, but it seems this house has a portal within it. How do I know? I recorded it. The clip is called "portal sound." What is heard is, well...absence of sound and atmosphere. No air, just space alone. My words where without substance, as I clearly heard the tick-tock of the grandfather clock in the other room, but seemed to be next to me as I felt the pressure that surrounded me making me feel pressed into the chair as if I was strapped in.

Darklands Paranormal was born in 2011, we found that our energy together produced the best photographic and audio evidence you will ever see and hear. We pulled hundreds of photos and class "A"

EVP's from mostly commercial buildings, enough to fill fifty albums on our website. In a four and a half year span we had been on "My Ghost Story" *Don't Fear the Creeper* and worked with Dream Works animation in 2012. We were going to be cartoon characters (that would have been fun) though nothing came of it, then we shot a pilot for SYFY in 2013. They loved us, but hated the other group they flew in from Texas. It went through the first green light, while Scott and I signed contracts to film the first episode, only to have them scrap it, stating they didn't like the concept. *But it was their idea?* That is Hollywood.

We were on Storage Wars; *Ghosts don't need no money* in 2014 because the producer wanted to film in a real haunted place which we had access to any time we wanted. We shot a sizzle reel for Sam Mettler, the guy who still produces the show *Intervention.* That was pretty cool for two reasons. We both were paid five-hundred dollars for a day's work, and the photographic subject matter was our own evidence presented to a group of skeptic people at The Center for Inquiry, in Hollywood. They tried to disprove the validity of Scott's" Time Machine" capture we have on film, they were not able to debunk it, and a piece of my audio of a real ghost speaking, they wanted nothing to do with that. If that show would have been picked up, we would have shot the first episode. The History Channel and SYFY were interested, but nothing came of that either.

I know now that the *Time Machine* was never meant to be shared with the public, that my friends, is an entirely different story.

Not only am I now finally ready to share the story of my life, of who I am and what I've become; it's just time. There will be hundreds of shocked people that know of me, that would never have thought I was born the opposite gender that I am now. There will be different reactions from different people whether they read this story, or better yet, if it becomes a movie. There was a time when a Hollywood producer saw a photo of me after he was told I was born female. He said, "Well that went well!" Then he called me and was perplexed at how great my voice was. I don't know what he was expecting. He went on to ask me if I would be available to be on set for three months straight, I told him sure.

Now he knew I was a paranormal investigator, and had an interest in such things, so when I had shared with him that I had access to a known haunted place in Texas, it piqued his interest. That is, until he *saw* the photo of me with the woman that gained me my access. Oh yes, he was even more interested now. So much so, he called me and said, "She is gorgeous! I need to speak with her on bringing a film crew out there!" The next thing I knew was they were communicating, she was telling him that she wanted me and Scott to do the filming with her, but he insisted he bring in another team of investigators, knowing she had a thing for me. When she would not back down from her demand, he proceeded to out my past to her, telling her I was born female. She flipped out, called him a liar, then called me crying wondering why I never told her. Why would I tell her something that made no difference in our working relationship? He wanted me out of his way, to be sure he had a clear path to the bedroom with her, and she would have gladly agreed in order to get what she wanted from him, which was her own show. This is Hollywood, and that was the end of what could have been a very big film for him.

All I really want to do now is help people like me at any stage of their life, or their transition. Also, to educate the masses of people that have no concept and certainly no understanding of what a transgendered person is, as complicated as it can be. There are so many misconceptions about people like us that I want to help clear up. There will be

many people who will identify with my story on one or many levels. "Boys Don't Cry" (Hillary Swank) 1999 is the only major movie I know of its kind dealing with the life of a transman, who unfortunately died because of who and what he was; just as I am.

Now is the time a new film is brought about on this subject, on the rises and the falls of us who were born to be as we are, along with the importance of becoming triumphant over the very things that made us not fit the societal mold that has been put forth since the beginning of time.